Le[illegible] from the Story of Yūsuf

عَلَيۡهِ ٱلسَّلَامُ

By Shaykh ‘Abd ur-Raḥmān ibn Nāṣir as-Sa’dī

DuSunnah Publication, United Kingdom

ISNB: 978-09929123-0-7
Paperback

فوائد مستنبطة من

قصة يوسف

عليه السلام

تأليف

العلامة الشيخ عبد الرحمن بن ناصر السعدي

المتوفى سنة ١٣٧٦هـ

Lessons Learnt from the Story of Yūsuf

First Published in Great Britain, April 2014CE | Jumadá al-Ākhar 1435H

Published by: DuSunnah Publications – Masjid Daar us Sunnah, Lime Grove, Shepherds Bush, London W12 8DE **Email:** Admin@DuSunnah.com **Tel:** 0208 749 6187

Website: www.DuSunnah.com
Online Shop: www.DuSunnahBookshop.com
Live Broadcast: Live.DuSunnah.com
Video: Video.DuSunnah.com
Twitter: @DaarusSunnah

Translated by: Abū ʻAbdillāh Nūr ad-Dīn

Cover and Interior Design by: Pario Studio - www.ParioStudio.com | Info@pariostudio.com

ISNB: 978-0-9929123-1-4
Paperback

British Library Cataloguing in Publication Data
A catalogue record for this book is available from the British Library
First Edition: Great Britain, April 2014CE | Jumadá al-Ākhar 1435H

Printed in Europe

System of Transliteration

Letter	Pronunciation	Transliteration
ء	*hamza*	’
ا	*alif*	*ā*
ب	*bā’*	*b*
ت	*tā’*	*t*
ث	*thā’*	*th*
ج	*jīm*	*j*
ح	*ḥā’*	*ḥ*
خ	*kha*	*kh*
د	*dāl*	*d*
ذ	*dh*	*dh*
ر	*rā’*	*r*
ز	*zāy*	*z*
س	*sīn*	*s*
ش	*shīn*	*sh*
ص	*ṣād*	*ṣ*
ض	*ḍād*	*ḍ*
ط	*ṭā’*	*ṭ*
ظ	*ẓā’*	*ẓ*
ع	*‘ain*	‘
غ	*ġain*	*ġ*
ف	*fā’*	*f*
ق	*qāf*	*q*
ك	*kāf*	*k*
ل	*lām*	*l*
م	*mīm*	*m*
ن	*nūn*	*n*
ه	*hā’*	*h*
و	*wāw*	*ū*
ي	*yā’*	*ī*

بسم الله الرحمن الرحيم

With the name of Allāh, the One with All-Encompassing mercy,
who bestows His mercy on whoever He pleases, [I begin],

قائمة المحتويات

Table of Contents

التقديم

Publishers Preface

All praise belongs to Allāh (تَبَارَكَ وَتَعَالَى), the One who guides whichever of His slaves He pleases to the secrets of His revelation, the One who showed the ways to His grace using the best form of explanation, the One who gave His last Messenger the keys to effective communication, and the One who revealed His greatest book in the clear tongue of an Arab nation.

May Allāh (تَبَارَكَ وَتَعَالَى) raise the repute of His greatest Messenger and save him from every deficiency, the one He sent to remove people from the darkness and bring them into the light, the one who destroyed the confederates of disbelief by His will and His might, the one with whom He completed his proof against the disbelievers and sealed their plight, and the one whom He sent with the best of speech to separate the wrong from the right.

As for the topic of our discussion, it is but a short preface to the translation of a small but beneficial treatise written by the eminent and erudite scholar, Shaykh 'Abd ur-Raḥmān ibn Nāṣir as-Sa'dī, entitled: *Lessons Learnt from the Story of Yusuf.*

In it, he endeavours to outline numerous lessons, morals and principles that he extracted from the details of this great story, which will serve every Muslim both in his worship and his occupation, and both in his self and his interactions. We have taken this treatise and tried our best to translate it into a language that will make it easy for English speakers to understand, so that many people can benefit who would otherwise have been denied these wonderful fruits plucked by the eminent Shaykh for our consumption. We cannot recommend it enough. It is packed full of benefit as to warrant its own study and exposition, as is customary amongst the scholars of our noble religion. At the very least, we urge the reader to go through the book three or five times, or seven, or more, in order to properly absorb the knowledge being disseminated within.

To those well versed in the vast and beautiful language of the Arabs, it is well know that any translation of any work into English must necessarily fall short of the original in its beauty and delivery, as well as its depth of meaning. For a successful translation into English, one must add here and subtract there, so that one may render a translation that reads fluidly and easily but still preserves the original meaning intended by the author. Sometimes, one must expound in English where a few words in Arabic would have sufficed.

Even though we have endeavored to make it easy, it is inevitable that some language in this book may require a quick browse through the glossary, because the depth of meaning of some words in Arabic cannot be captured in English except with a word of higher complexity than normal. Sometimes, only a phrase or sentence will suffice! However, we have tried to keep it to a minimum.

In conclusion, we would like to apologies in advance for any mistakes or shortcomings that may have occurred in this translation. We hope that Allāh (تَبَارَكَ وَتَعَالَى) has helped us keep them to a minimum. Whatever the esteemed reader finds in it that is good is from Allāh (تَبَارَكَ وَتَعَالَى) alone, and that which is bad is from us and from shaytān, and we seek Allāh's (تَبَارَكَ وَتَعَالَى) forgiveness.

May Allāh (تَبَارَكَ وَتَعَالَى) raise the repute of his noble prophet, his family and his companions and save them from all forms of deficiency, and all praise is due to Allāh the Most High and the Ever Wise who always puts things in their proper place.

Masjid Daar us Sunnah
Monday 7th April 2014CE / 7th Jumadá al-Ākhar 1435H
London,
England.

ترجمة

A Biography of the Author

His name is Abū 'Abdillah 'Abd ur-Raḥmān ibn Nāṣir ibn 'Abdillāh ibn Nāṣir as-Sa'dī from Āl as-Sa'dī, the Shaykh, descended of the Tamīm tribe. He was born in the town of 'Unaizah in al-Qaṣīm on the 12th of *Muḥarram* in the year 1307H. His mother died when he was four years old, and his father died when he was seven. As a result, he grew up an orphan but he had a stable upbringing.

He had already attracted attention at a young age with his intelligence and his strong enthusiasm for learning. After the death of his father, he had read the Qur'ān, then thoroughly memorised it by the time he was eleven years old. Then he began learning from the learned men of his town and those who visited it. He worked hard until he acquired a respectable amount of knowledge in every field. When he reached the age of twenty-three, he began teaching. Like that, he used to both learn and teach, and the entirety of his time was spent doing that. It was like that until in the year 1351H, he was made in charge of education in his town, and became a mentor for all the students.

Some of the Shaykh's teachers:

He studied under Shaykh Ibrāhīm ibn Ḥamd ibn Jāsir. He was the first person he read to. He used give descriptions about his teacher's recollection of *ḥadīth*, and he would talk at length about his fear of Allāh (تَبَارَكَ وَتَعَالَى) and his love of sharing with the poor despite his lack of means. Often, a poor person would come to him on a cold winter's day and he would strip himself of one of his pair of garments from his own poverty and dress him in it - despite his own needs.

Another one of the author's teachers is Shaykh Muḥammad ibn 'Abd al-Karīm ash-Shibl. With him, he studied *Fiqh*, Arabic sciences and other subjects. From amongst his teachers was also Ṣāliḥ ibn 'Uthmān, the judge of 'Unaizah, with whom he studied *Tawhīd*, *Tafsīr*, the principles of *Fiqh* as well as its various branches, and Arabic sciences. It was with him that the author studied most, and he stuck with him earnestly until his death.

Other teachers include Shaykh 'Abdullāh ibn 'Ayiḍh, Shaykh Sā'id at-Tuwaijirī, Shaykh, 'Ali'ī ibn as-Sinānī, Shaykh, 'Ali'ī Nāṣir, Shaykh Abū Wādī – with whom he studied *ḥadīth*, the six major books and others, and who gave him a teaching endorsement for them. Mentioned amongst his teachers is also Muhammad, the son of Shaykh 'Abdul al-'Azīz al-Muhammad al-Mānī', KSA Director of education at the time – the author studied with him in 'Unaizah. Shaykh Muḥammad al-Mukhtār ash-Shiniqīṭī - resident of *al-ḥijāz* back in the day and afterwards, Zubayr – was also one of his teachers. He came to 'Unaizah and remained there in order to teach. At that time, the author learnt from him *Tafsīr*, *ḥadīth*, and Arabic sciences such as Grammar, Morphology, and the like.

A Little Bit about the Author's Character:

He possessed many exceptional virtues. He was humble to the young and the old, the rich and the poor. He used to spend his time meeting the people who desired his company. Their gatherings were circles of knowledge for the reason that his endeavour was to make them consist of congregational study and research, and bring huge benefits, through these useful and time-consuming studies, to the people who attended the sessions. Normal get-togethers would turn into study sessions and worship. He would converse with each individual according to his needs, and together they would look at his religious and material interests. He would often settle disputes that ended with both of the parties being satisfied with his fair mediation.

He used to have compassion for the poor, the needy and the outsider, lending them a helping hand whenever he could. Whenever the opportunity arose, he would appeal to those whom he knew loved to support a good cause.

He used to be a man of exceptional etiquette, modesty, integrity and determination in all of his duties. He was the best of instructors and the most effective of people in clarifying a matter. He organised the class schedules and he would arrange debates between his accomplished students in order to stimulate their minds; he would offer a prize to whoever could memorise some of the textbooks, and he would give the prize to everyone who managed to memorise them without leaving anyone out.

He used to consult with his students over the most helpful books to study, consenting to the wishes of the majority or making the choice himself if there was no clear favourite. The students never tired of his long lectures - whenever they were long – because of how much they enjoyed his company, which is why he had and still has so many accomplished students. I pray that Allāh (تَبَارَكَ وَتَعَالَى) gives him a gratifying life and blesses us all with abundance in our time and furnishes us with good deeds that will serve us forever.

The Author's Academic Calibre:

He had extensive knowledge of *Fiqh*, both its theoretical and practical aspects. In the beginning he, following in the footsteps of his teachers, adhered to the *Ḥanbalī* school of thought and memorised some of its textbooks. Around the time, he authored a book on the subject of *Fiqh* consisting of about 400 verses of poetry based on the *Rajz* poetic metre and concisely explained it. However, he did not wish for it to be published because it was based on his views from his first days as a student.

His greatest preoccupation was with the books of Shaykh al-Islām Ibn Taimiyyah and his student, Ibn al-Qayyim, which were also his greatest influences. They did him a lot of good in terms of learning fundamental principles, *Tawḥīd*, *Tafsīr*, *Fiqh*, as well as other useful subjects. Due to the insight he gained from the two aforementioned scholars, he became unattached to any particular school of thought. Instead, what he considered the strongest opinion on a matter would be the one supported by legitimate proof. Yet he would not speak ill against the scholars of the various schools the way some confused people do, may Allāh (تَبَارَكَ وَتَعَالَى) guide them along with us to the proper path.

He was highly accomplished in the field of *Tafsīr*, having read many works of various scholars. He excelled in it and himself authored an important book of *Tafsīr* consisting of many volumes. He wrote it spontaneously, without there being a single book of *Tafsīr* or any other book present with him at the time. Consistently, he would read the Qur'ān with the students and explain it offhand without prior preparation. He would branch into different topics and clarify some of the meanings of the Qur'ān and mention some of its lessons. He would deduce its inimitable benefits and important concepts, to such an extent that his listener would wish for him to prolong because of his eloquence, the wealth of his vocabulary and his elaborate discussion of evidences and stories. Whoever shared his company, read to him and researched with him realised his high academic calibre. The same goes for anyone who reads his books and legal verdicts.

Some of the Author's Academic Works:

1. An exegesis of the Noble Qur'ān titled *Taysīr al-Karīm al-Mannān* (A Facilitation from the Generous, the Gracious), in eight volumes. He completed it in 1344^H. It was never published.

2. *Irshād ulil-Basāīr wal al-Bāb li-Mā'rifatil Fiqh bī Aqrabīt Turuq wa Aisar il-Asbāb* (A Guide to Understanding *Fiqh* for the Insightful and Intelligent in the Shortest Time and Easiest Steps), arranged in question & answer format and printed by a Turkish printing house in Damascus in 1365^H, paid for by the author and distributed for free.

3. *al-Durrah al-Mukhtaṣarah fī Maḥāsin al-Dīn al-Islāmī* printed by *Anṣār us Sunnah* Press in 1366^H.

4. *al-Khūṭub al-'Aṣriyyah al-Qayyimah* (A Priceless Collection of Sermons on Contemporary Issues); when he became responsible for giving sermons in his town, he endeavoured to give, every *'Eid* and *Jumū'ah,* sermons on important topics that were relevant to the season and necessary to the people. Afterwards, paying for it himself, he compiled them, and together with *ad-Dūrratūl Mūkhtasarah*, they were printed by *Anṣār usSunnah* Press and distributed for free.

5. *al-Qawā'id al-Ḥisān li-Tafsīr al-Qur'ān* (Excellent Principles for Explaining the Qur'ān), printed by *Anṣār us Sunnah* Press in 1366^H and distributed for free.

6. *Wujūd at-Ta' āwun bayn al-Muslimin wal- Ādhul Jihād ad-Dīn* (Cooperation Amongst Muslims as a Duty, and the Subject of Religious Campaign).

The last three books above were printed by *As-Salafiyyah* printing press in Cairo with the author's funding and distributed for free.

7. *al-Qawl as-Sadīd fī Maqāṣid al-Tawḥīd* (The Truth About the Objectives of *Tawḥīd*), 1367^H - printed in Egypt by *al-Imām* Printing Press press and paid for by Abd al-Muḥsin Abū Baṭīn.

8. *Taysīr al-Laṭīf al-Mannān fī Khulāṣat Tafsīr al-Qur'ān* (A Facilitation from The Kind, The Gracious: A Digest of Qur'ānic Exegesis), *al-Imām* Printing Press. The author, along with a group of charitable people, paid for its printing and distributed it for free.

He also has many useful widely-circulated remarks and many verdicts taken from his answers to questions that came to him from his town and other places. He has various notes on the contents of many of the books he came across. He used to find it extremely easy to write, to the extent that he wrote down a great number of verdicts, amongst other things.

Why He Wrote:

His main purpose in writing was to disseminate knowledge and call people to the truth. This is why he compiled, wrote and printed as much as he was able to of his works, not gaining any transient or material compensation, but rather, distributing them for free so that anyone and everyone could benefit from them. I pray that Allāh (تَبَارَكَ وَتَعَالَى) rewards him kindly for his service to Islām and the Muslims, and makes it possible for us to do things that please him.

His Death:

After a blessed life of almost 69 years spent entirely in the service of knowledge, he left to be closer to his Lord in the year 1376^{H}, in the city of 'Unaizah, part of the land of al-Qaṣīm, may Allāh (تَبَارَكَ وَتَعَالَى) show him abundant mercy.

المقدمة

Introduction

All praise belongs and is due to Allāh (تَبَارَكَ وَتَعَالَىٰ) alone, and may Allāh raise the repute of Muḥammad (صَلَّى ٱللَّهُ عَلَيْهِ وَسَلَّمَ) and shower his family and companions with his mercy.

As for what follows:

These are some insights gained from the story of Yūsuf (عَلَيْهِ ٱلسَّلَامُ), may Allāh raise his repute and the repute of all the prophets and messengers.

Indeed, Allāh (تَبَارَكَ وَتَعَالَىٰ) related the story to us in detail, and said at the end of it:

﴿ لَقَدْ كَانَ فِي قَصَصِهِمْ عِبْرَةٌ لِّأُولِي ٱلْأَلْبَٰبِ ﴾

"Indeed in their stories, there is a lesson for men of understanding."

[*Sūrah Yūsuf* 12:111]

A “lesson” is something by which one learns. It steers a person towards a number of ideas and useful principles. It directs a person towards things that are virtuous, and alerts one to the causes of destruction.

While all stories of the prophets are like that, Allāh (تَبَارَكَ وَتَعَالَىٰ) singled this story out with His words:

﴿ لَّقَدْ كَانَ فِي يُوسُفَ وَإِخْوَتِهِۦٓ ءَايَٰتٌ لِّلسَّآئِلِينَ ۝٧ ﴾

“Truly, there are signs and lessons in [the story] of Yūsuf and his brothers for those asking [about the story of Yūsuf or for signs of the prophethood of Muḥammad].”

[*Sūrah Yūsuf* 12:7]

As such, it contains various signs and lessons for anyone who asks for them and seeks guidance and integrity. This is due to what it contains of one evolving circumstance to another; from one ordeal to another; from facing challenges to being blessed; from humiliation and slavery to honour and authority; from division to unity and fulfilled aspirations; from grief to joy; from abundance to scarcity, from scarcity to abundance, from famine to plenitude and from hardship to ease, amongst the other things this great story embodies. So blessed be the one who narrated it, clarified it and explained it.

‘Abd ur-Raḥmān ibn Nāṣir ibn Ṣa’dī

(رَحِمَهُ ٱللَّهُ)

The Fundamentals of Dream Interpretation

One benefit of this chapter is that it contains the fundamental principles of dream interpretation. This is [a benefit] because the science of dream interpretation is a vast and important science built upon excellent understanding, and the analysis of words and tangible and intangible phenomena, or such similar occurrences, while giving due consideration to the personal condition of the dreamer, the time of day, and the circumstances associated with the dream.

It can be seen how Allāh (تَبَارَكَ وَتَعَالَى) has praised Yūsuf (عَلَيْهِ السَّلَامُ) for his knowledge of the interpretation of languages – interpretation of the language of the rules and regulations of [Islamic] law and the language associated with dream interpretation. There is a difference between a genuine dream and muddled visions that have no valid explanation, like the ones seen by a person who thinks about and contemplates a particular issue for a long time, for it is true that he will often see in his sleep a variety of what he was thinking about while he was awake. As a result, the majority of these types of dreams are in fact muddled visions that have no explanation.

Another type is the false visions and confused messages that the devil casts into the subconscious of the sleeping person. This type, also, has no explanation, and it is improper for an intelligent person to preoccupy himself with it. Rather, he should pay no attention to it.

As for the genuine type of dream: it is inspiration with which Allāh (تَبَارَكَ وَتَعَالَىٰ) inspires a soul during the period of the soul's separation from the body. It may also be parables and analogies that the angel constructs for the human being in order for him to understand things comparable to them. It is also possible that he would see something and the interpretation would turn out to be exactly what he saw in his sleep. Allāh (تَبَارَكَ وَتَعَالَىٰ) gave Yūsuf (عَلَيْهِ ٱلسَّلَامُ) the knowledge to differentiate between genuine visions and fake ones, and to differentiate between the truth and the lies within them. This story contains many instances of the evidence for the interpretation of dreams. One of them is Yūsuf's (عَلَيْهِ ٱلسَّلَامُ) dream, which he told his father Ya'qūb (عَلَيْهِ ٱلسَّلَامُ):

﴿ إِذْ قَالَ يُوسُفُ لِأَبِيهِ يَٰٓأَبَتِ إِنِّي رَأَيْتُ أَحَدَ عَشَرَ كَوْكَبًا وَٱلشَّمْسَ وَٱلْقَمَرَ رَأَيْتُهُمْ لِي سَٰجِدِينَ ﴿٤﴾ ﴾

"[Remember] when Yūsuf said to his father, "My dear father! Verily, I saw (in a dream) eleven stars and the sun and the moon, I saw them prostrating themselves to me!"

[*Sūrah Yūsuf* 12:4]

Ya'qūb (عَلَيْهِ ٱلسَّلَامُ) then explained it by referring to its culmination, how it would all turn out, and the things that would lead to that. He interpreted the sun and the moon to be Yūsuf's father (عَلَيْهِ ٱلسَّلَامُ) and mother respectively, and the eleven stars to be his brothers, and that eventually and undoubtedly, they would all prostrate to Yūsuf

(عَلَيْهِ ٱلسَّلَامُ) and humble themselves before him. That is why when they were reunited, and his father, mother and brothers came to Egypt and he raised his father and mother onto the throne, all of them fell in prostration to him, and Yūsuf (عَلَيْهِ ٱلسَّلَامُ) said, remembering this interpretation:

﴿ وَقَالَ يَٰٓأَبَتِ هَٰذَا تَأْوِيلُ رُءْيَٰىَ مِن قَبْلُ قَدْ جَعَلَهَا رَبِّى حَقًّا ۝١٠٠ ﴾

"He said: This is the interpretation of my dream aforetime! My Lord has made it come true!"

[*Sūrah Yūsuf* 12:100]

This was an extraordinary development – that Yūsuf's (عَلَيْهِ ٱلسَّلَامُ) situation reached the point where he was deeply admired by his parents and brothers, as well as by the people. An outcome like this requires facilitators and precursors without which it cannot occur. These are, namely, having a vast amount of knowledge, doing virtuous deeds, being sincerely devoted to Allāh (تَبَارَكَ وَتَعَالَىٰ), being chosen and appointed by Him, and fulfilling one's obligations towards Allāh (تَبَارَكَ وَتَعَالَىٰ) and His creatures. This is why He (تَبَارَكَ وَتَعَالَىٰ) said, while mentioning the factors that lead to this wonderful outcome,

﴿ وَكَذَٰلِكَ يَجْتَبِيكَ رَبُّكَ وَيُعَلِّمُكَ مِن تَأْوِيلِ ٱلْأَحَادِيثِ وَيُتِمُّ نِعْمَتَهُۥ عَلَيْكَ وَعَلَىٰٓ ءَالِ
يَعْقُوبَ كَمَآ أَتَمَّهَا عَلَىٰٓ أَبَوَيْكَ مِن قَبْلُ إِبْرَٰهِيمَ وَإِسْحَٰقَ ۚ إِنَّ رَبَّكَ عَلِيمٌ حَكِيمٌ ۝٦ ﴾

"And thus will your Lord choose you, teach you the interpretation of dreams and give you His full blessing and on the offspring of Ya'qūb (Jacob), just as He gave it before to both your forefathers Ibrāhīm and Isḥāq, truly your Lord is All-Knowing, Most Wise."

[*Sūrah Yūsuf* 12:6]

That is, Allāh (تَبَارَكَ وَتَعَالَى) will grant you His full blessing by teaching you useful knowledge and virtuous deeds; by choosing you, and by helping you develop beautiful qualities and attain positions of high office. He gave him glad tidings that these events would occur, and that thereafter he would achieve a high standing in this life and the next.

This interpretation by Ya'qūb (عَلَيْهِ السَّلَامُ) comprises glad tidings for Yūsuf (عَلَيْهِ السَّلَامُ) and consolation for the hardship and suffering he would receive at the hands of his brothers and in prison. For, no doubt, if a person knows that hardships and adversities will lead to blessings and ease, he is comforted and he will find it easy to bear their difficulties and effects. This news was a great kindness and a huge relief for him. This is included in the kindness to which Yūsuf (عَلَيْهِ السَّلَامُ) indicated with his words:

﴿إِنَّ رَبِّي لَطِيفٌ لِّمَا يَشَآءُ إِنَّهُۥ هُوَ ٱلْعَلِيمُ ٱلْحَكِيمُ﴾

"Certainly, my Lord is the Most Kind unto whom He wills. He is the All-Knowing, the All-Wise."

[*Sūrah Yūsuf* 12:100]

Allāh's (تَبَارَكَ وَتَعَالَى) wisdom dictates that noble positions cannot be attained except through noble means, and this is why He said:

﴿إِنَّ رَبَّكَ عَلِيمٌ حَكِيمٌ﴾

"Truly, your Lord is All-Knowing, Most-Wise."

[*Sūrah Yūsuf* 12:6].

Glad Tidings for Ya'qūb and Yūsuf's Mother and Brothers

Amongst the insights gained from this interpretation of Yūsuf's (عَلَيْهِ ٱلسَّلَامُ) dream is the tremendously good news it heralds for Ya'qūb (عَلَيْهِ ٱلسَّلَامُ), Yūsuf's mother and his brothers of the prestige, righteousness and good they will achieve. Hence, Ya'qūb (عَلَيْهِ ٱلسَّلَامُ) is one of the greatest prophets and one of the best of those chosen by Allāh (تَبَارَكَ وَتَعَالَىٰ). His (Yūsuf's عَلَيْهِ ٱلسَّلَامُ) mother is quite virtuous and has prestige in this life and the next, since she was compared to the sun, or the moon – according to two different opinions.

As for his brothers, although they deeply hurt both their father and brother through disobedience and cutting the ties of kinship, both of them forgave them, overlooked their actions, and sought forgiveness from Allāh (تَبَارَكَ وَتَعَالَىٰ) for them, and Allāh (تَبَارَكَ وَتَعَالَىٰ) is the most Merciful of those who are merciful. The sun, moon and stars all incorporate light and elevation, each one varying from the other in the intensity of its light and the distance of its elevation. These variations correspond to the differences in virtue between the parents and the brothers.

In summary, this dream truly embodies the materialisation of the good of this life and the hereafter for Yūsuf (عَلَيْهِ السَّلَامُ). It includes the lofty positions he attained, the factors that lead to them, all the bounties that these events brought, and the fact that his parents and brothers would be sharing with him in the blessings of this life and the next; and Allāh (تَبَارَكَ وَتَعَالَى) knows best.

The Dream of the Two Young Men

As for the dreams of the two young men, when one of them said:

﴿إِنِّيٓ أَرَىٰنِيٓ أَعۡصِرُ خَمۡرٗاۖ وَقَالَ ٱلۡأٓخَرُ إِنِّيٓ أَرَىٰنِيٓ أَحۡمِلُ فَوۡقَ رَأۡسِي خُبۡزٗا تَأۡكُلُ ٱلطَّيۡرُ مِنۡهُۖ ٣٦﴾

"Verily, I saw myself (in a dream) pressing wine." The other said: "Verily, I saw myself (in a dream) carrying bread on my head and birds were eating thereof."

[*Sūrah Yūsuf* 12:36]

They saw how good Yūsuf was (عَلَيۡهِ ٱلسَّلَامُ) with everything and how benevolent he acted towards Allāh's (تَبَارَكَ وَتَعَالَىٰ) creatures, and because of this, they kindly asked him to interpret their dreams for them. He subsequently interpreted the dream of the one who saw himself pressing grapes to mean that he would be freed from his imprisonment and return to his former status and be at the service of his master, after which he would press for him the grapes that would become wine. He interpreted the second one's dream to mean that he would be killed, then crucified, and then have birds peck at his head. Therefore, the first one's dream was literal. On the other hand, the second one's dream was symbolic - that he would in fact be killed, as well as crucified and would not be buried until birds pecked at his head. This interpretation shows Yūsuf's incredible understanding and ability to uncover hidden meanings, because common practice is that once a person is killed, he is buried immediately, preventing beasts of prey and birds from eating his remains. This is why he understood that this man would be executed and not buried right away, but would be left unburied until he ended up in that state. This punishment involves much shame and disgrace, and such a brutal end to his [current] worldly life that it makes the skin crawl. Yūsuf, knowing that these genuine dreams would undoubtedly come true, said to them:

﴿ قُضِىَ ٱلْأَمْرُ ٱلَّذِى فِيهِ تَسْتَفْتِيَانِ ﴾

"Thus is the case judged concerning which you both did inquire."

[*Sūrah Yūsuf* 12:41]

This is because of his full knowledge of dream interpretation, whereby he does not interpret by relying on guesses or misconceptions, but rather interprets using knowledge and certainty. As for the rationale behind the interpretation, it is that birds do not approach the living, and they only feed on a dead person's remains when there is no one around him. This would only happen after he had been killed and crucified.

Another instance that reveals Yūsuf's (عَلَيْهِ ٱلسَّلَامُ) excellence, earnestness and his remarkable understanding is that when the two men told him their dreams, he delayed the interpretation of their dreams while promising them that he would inform them of it in due time. He told them:

﴿ قَالَ لَا يَأْتِيكُمَا طَعَامٌ تُرْزَقَانِهِۦٓ إِلَّا نَبَّأْتُكُمَا بِتَأْوِيلِهِۦ قَبْلَ أَن يَأْتِيَكُمَا ﴿٣٧﴾ ﴾

"No food will come to you (in wakefulness or in dream) as your provision, but I will inform (in wakefulness) its interpretation before it (the food) comes."

[*Sūrah Yūsuf* 12:37]

He promised to interpret their dreams before the first meal they would receive from outside the prison, so that they would be at ease and look forward to the interpretations, and so that he would be able to preach to them before that. This would make it more likely for them to answer the call to Allāh (تَبَارَكَ وَتَعَالَىٰ), their invitation to Allāh (تَبَارَكَ وَتَعَالَىٰ) being more important than the interpretation of their dreams. He then called them to Allāh (تَبَارَكَ وَتَعَالَىٰ) using two arguments:

Firstly: by referring to his personal condition and how the beautiful qualities he possessed helped him attain such a prestigious position, saying:

﴿ ذَٰلِكُمَا مِمَّا عَلَّمَنِي رَبِّيٓۚ إِنِّي تَرَكۡتُ مِلَّةَ قَوۡمٖ لَّا يُؤۡمِنُونَ بِٱللَّهِ وَهُم بِٱلۡأٓخِرَةِ هُمۡ كَٰفِرُونَ
٣٧ وَٱتَّبَعۡتُ مِلَّةَ ءَابَآءِيٓ إِبۡرَٰهِيمَ وَإِسۡحَٰقَ وَيَعۡقُوبَۚ مَا كَانَ لَنَآ أَن نُّشۡرِكَ بِٱللَّهِ مِن
شَيۡءٖۚ ذَٰلِكَ مِن فَضۡلِ ٱللَّهِ عَلَيۡنَا وَعَلَى ٱلنَّاسِ وَلَٰكِنَّ أَكۡثَرَ ٱلنَّاسِ لَا يَشۡكُرُونَ ٣٨ ﴾

"That is some of what my Lord taught me, indeed I abandoned the religion of people who do not believe in Allāh and are disbelievers in the hereafter (i.e. the Kan'aniun of Egypt who were polytheists and used to worship sun and other false deities). And I followed the religion of my fathers, Ibrāhīm, Isḥāq and Ya'qūb. We would never associate anything at all with Allāh; that is Allāh's grace towards us and the people, yet most people do not show any gratitude."

[*Sūrah Yūsuf* 12:37-38]

Secondly: he persuaded them using legitimate, intuitive arguments –

﴿ يَٰصَٰحِبَيِ ٱلسِّجۡنِ ءَأَرۡبَابٞ مُّتَفَرِّقُونَ خَيۡرٌ أَمِ ٱللَّهُ ٱلۡوَٰحِدُ ٱلۡقَهَّارُ ٣٩ مَا تَعۡبُدُونَ
مِن دُونِهِۦٓ إِلَّآ أَسۡمَآءٗ سَمَّيۡتُمُوهَآ أَنتُمۡ وَءَابَآؤُكُم مَّآ أَنزَلَ ٱللَّهُ بِهَا مِن سُلۡطَٰنٍۚ إِنِ
ٱلۡحُكۡمُ إِلَّا لِلَّهِۚ أَمَرَ أَلَّا تَعۡبُدُوٓاْ إِلَّآ إِيَّاهُۚ ذَٰلِكَ ٱلدِّينُ ٱلۡقَيِّمُ وَلَٰكِنَّ أَكۡثَرَ ٱلنَّاسِ لَا
يَعۡلَمُونَ ٤٠ ﴾

"My Fellow prisoners! Are many different lords better or Allāh the One, the All-Subduing? All that you worship besides Him are nothing but names you and your fathers adopted with no authorisation sent down from Allāh. The mandate is for no one except Allāh. He ordered that you should worship no one besides Him. That is the correct religion, but most people do not know."

[*Sūrah Yūsuf* 12:39-40]

for the One who is alone in His (تَبَارَكَ وَتَعَالَى) Perfection in all aspects, and in His (تَبَارَكَ وَتَعَالَى) Subjugation of the heavenly and netherworlds, the One who has the right to total divinity, the One who created all creatures to worship him and commanded them as such, and the One to whom belongs the authority over His (تَبَارَكَ وَتَعَالَى) slaves in this life and the hereafter. He (تَبَارَكَ وَتَعَالَى) alone, and no one else, deserves worship to the exclusion of everything else - to whom worship is due, to the exclusion of the varying, deficient gods for whom every nation claims divinity, even though they possess neither essence of divinity nor merit. In fact, they are merely names they agreed to adopt; names without meaning.

Yūsuf decided that their invitation to Allāh (تَبَارَكَ وَتَعَالَى) took precedence over the interpretation of their dreams, and was of more benefit to them as well as other people.

As for the King's dream:

In fact, he saw seven emaciated cows eating seven plump cows, and seven shrivelled, fragile ears of grain eating and demolishing seven green ears, and it terrified him! So, he gathered all those whom he thought possessed expertise, yet none of them knew its interpretation, and they said:

﴿ قَالُوٓاْ أَضۡغَٰثُ أَحۡلَٰمٖۖ وَمَا نَحۡنُ بِتَأۡوِيلِ ٱلۡأَحۡلَٰمِ بِعَٰلِمِينَ ﴾

"[These are] mixed up false dreams and we are not skilled in the interpretation of dreams."

[*Sūrah Yūsuf* 12:44]

After that, the man who was released from prison recalled his memories of Yūsuf and his vast knowledge - and his knowledge of dream interpretation. He also remembered Yūsuf's (عَلَيۡهِ ٱلسَّلَامُ) request, which the devil caused him forget to mention to his master, the [divine] wisdom behind which had become clear – that he (Yūsuf عَلَيۡهِ ٱلسَّلَامُ) would not leave prison until after his widespread renown and his interpretation of the king's dream had shown his clear superiority over everyone else. This man then requested of the king to send him to Yūsuf (عَلَيۡهِ ٱلسَّلَامُ), and guaranteed the people that he would return with the correct interpretation of the dream.

So when he came to Yūsuf (عَلَيۡهِ ٱلسَّلَامُ), he said to him:

﴿ يُوسُفُ أَيُّهَا ٱلصِّدِّيقُ أَفۡتِنَا فِي سَبۡعِ بَقَرَٰتٖ سِمَانٖ يَأۡكُلُهُنَّ سَبۡعٌ عِجَافٞ وَسَبۡعِ سُنۢبُلَٰتٍ خُضۡرٖ وَأُخَرَ يَابِسَٰتٖ لَّعَلِّيٓ أَرۡجِعُ إِلَى ٱلنَّاسِ لَعَلَّهُمۡ يَعۡلَمُونَ ٤٦ ﴾

"O' Yūsuf (Joseph), man of truth! Explain to us (the dream) of seven fat cows whom seven lean ones were devouring, and of seven green ears of corn, and (seven) others dry, that I may return to the people, and that they may know."

[*Sūrah Yūsuf* 12:46]

Because the king and the people have sent me to you in order for you to interpret it, and they very eagerly await your interpretation. This is why he said,

﴿ يَا بِسَبِ لَعَلِّيٓ أَرۡجِعُ إِلَى ٱلنَّاسِ لَعَلَّهُمۡ يَعۡلَمُونَ ﴾

"That I may return to the people, and that they may know."

[*Sūrah Yūsuf* 12:46]

That is, so that they may know that which worried, terrified and tormented the king.

Yūsuf (عَلَيۡهِ ٱلسَّلَامُ) then interpreted it immediately, and added to his interpretation the best course of action to be taken regarding the dream and the best way to manage its implications. He informed them that the plump cows and the seven green ears of grain would be consecutive years of ease and abundance that would precede the years of drought and infertility. The emaciated cows and shrivelled ears of grain were the years of drought and barrenness that would follow. He told them that after these years, a year would come in which people would be relieved by abundant rain and will press [wine and oil]. He added that during the years of abundance they should take the opportunity to earnestly prepare for the years of hardship, and should sow an enormous amount of crop, much more than the usual amount, which is why he said:

﴿ تَزْرَعُونَ سَبْعَ سِنِينَ ﴾

"For seven consecutive years."

[*Sūrah Yūsuf* 12:47]

Obviously, people plant every year in any case, but what he meant here was for them to produce a great deal of crop and exhaust their resources in growing all that they could. Furthermore, they should take precautions regarding the produce when it is ready, by storing it and economising it, so he said:

﴿ فَمَا حَصَدتُّمْ فَذَرُوهُ فِي سُنۢبُلِهِۦٓ إِلَّا قَلِيلًا مِّمَّا تَأْكُلُونَ ﴾

"And that (the harvest) which you reap you shall leave in ears, (all) - except a little of it which you may eat.."

[*Sūrah Yūsuf* 12:47]

That is, they should preserve the harvest in a way that would keep it safe from spoilage and moth-worms (and the like), by leaving the grain in its ears; and they should economise during this period – the period of ease – and not use too much of the grain, but rather they should eat a little and save a lot. Then after these years of abundance, they would experience years of drought and hardship that would involve all the Egyptian territories and surrounding areas, and these years would see the consumption of what was saved in preparation for them from the years of abundance:

﴿ لَهُنَّ إِلَّا قَلِيلًا مِّمَّا تُحْصِنُونَ ﴾

"Except a little of it which you may eat.."

[*Sūrah Yūsuf* 12:48]

The rationale behind this interpretation is that, as mentioned previously, a dream should be interpreted with due consideration for the dreamer's situation and the circumstances surrounding the dream. In this case, the dreamer is the king who is directly associated with the well being and general affairs of his subjects. This is why his dream applies not only to him but also to the people.

Now, the rationale behind interpreting the cows and ears of grain as years is obvious by looking at cows from two angles:

1. They are the most commonly used animal to plough the land; and cultivation, crop plantings and so on, depend on the years' rain or drought.

2. The cow is the kind of livestock whose plumpness or leanness depends on the condition during each year. Thus, when the years are fertile, they grow fat, and when the years are infertile and barren, they become thin and emaciated. Similar to that are ears of grain – grain production thrives and seedlings grow to their full capacity with the abundance of water and many years of fertility, and they wither and dry up during years of infertility and drought. Therefore, his dreams about cows and ears of grain were descriptions of the years and their effects, and a reference to means and their ends. That is, cultivating the fields is a means, and the growth of produce and fattening of livestock are the ends and intent behind that.

As for his statement:

﴿ ثُمَّ يَأْتِي مِنۢ بَعْدِ ذَٰلِكَ عَامٌ فِيهِ يُغَاثُ ٱلنَّاسُ وَفِيهِ يَعْصِرُونَ ﴾

"Then thereafter will come a year in which people will be saved and in which they will press (wine and oil).."

[*Sūrah Yūsuf* 12:49]

It means that during that year, people will receive rain that will rescue them from their drought. The fields will return to being fertile and their sterility will disappear. This deduction is based on the stipulation that the years of infertility were seven, for this stipulation shows that after these seven years an event will follow that will remove the hardships, drought and infertility of the previous years.

It is obvious that seven successive years of infertility would not leave the slightest trace of vegetation, plantation or seedlings on the land, and any land in such an extreme state of desolation cannot be restored except by a vast amount of rainfall. This is quite obvious, and Yūsuf deducted this fact from the king's dream. Yet, surprisingly, none of the explanations [of the Qur'ān] that I came across mentioned this implication, despite its clarity. Instead they said, perhaps some specific revelation came to Yūsuf (عَلَيْهِ ٱلسَّلَامُ) regarding this year during which people will receive rain and press [wine, oil, etc]. However, there is no need for what they mentioned, and actually – and to Allāh (تَبَارَكَ وَتَعَالَىٰ) alone all praise is due - this fact (that they will be saved by rain) is clear to see from what is implied by the number [i.e. seven].

It is also clear from the context, since he gave this interpretation as a clarification of the king's dream. One must also realise that the king's dream, Yūsuf's (عَلَيْهِ ٱلسَّلَامُ) interpretation of it and his outstanding supervision of the events that followed were a mercy from Allāh (تَبَارَكَ وَتَعَالَىٰ) to Yūsuf (عَلَيْهِ ٱلسَّلَامُ), the king and the people. Since, if it were not for this dream, Yūsuf's (عَلَيْهِ ٱلسَّلَامُ) interpretation, and his supervision thereafter, the years of drought would have taken the people by surprise before they had sufficiently prepared for them, and as a result, great harm would have befallen the entire Egyptian region and its neighbouring lands.

Therefore, this was a mercy to them and others [outside Egypt]. Look at how the drought covered the Egyptian lands, the Levant (*Shām*) and Palestinian lands, amongst others, until they needed rations from Egypt, and Yūsuf (عَلَيْهِ ٱلسَّلَامُ) had to calculate [rations] for everyone and distribute them in a way that would be fair and sympathetic to all and in a way that would be enough to sustain them.

Moreover, this great intelligence from Yūsuf (عَلَيْهِ ٱلسَّلَامُ) was the overwhelming reason for his exit from prison, and the reason for which the king brought him into his fold and made him his favourite, and for his full empowerment in the land to the extent that he could occupy it wherever he pleased. This was one of his acts of excellence, and Allāh (تَبَارَكَ وَتَعَالَىٰ) does not waste the reward of those who excel [in good deeds]. Despite the extent of this bounty, Allāh's (تَبَارَكَ وَتَعَالَىٰ) bounty is still much greater than that; He touches whomever He wills from amongst the people He chooses with His mercy, and He favours him with and gathers for him the good of both this world and the hereafter.

A Person Should Treat his Children Equally and with Fairness

Justice ensures their righteousness

It is necessary, if he happens to love one above the other[s], that he conceals his love as much as he is able to, and he should not give him preference, as love often dictates, in anything in particular. This is a wiser way to ensure their righteousness, ensure their reverence and respect for him, and to ensure that harmony exists between them.[1]

---

[1] Muslim (no.1623) and al-Bukhārī (no.2587) have cited this narration upon the authority of an-Nu'mān ibn Bashīr (رَضِيَ اللَّهُ عَنْهُ), who said:

> "My father gave me a gift, to which 'Amrá bint Ra'wāḥa said, I won't approve of this until you tell the Messenger of Allāh (صَلَّى اللَّهُ عَلَيْهِ وَسَلَّمَ) about it. So he went to the Messenger of Allāh (صَلَّى اللَّهُ عَلَيْهِ وَسَلَّمَ) and said; "I in fact gave my son through 'Amrá bint Ra'wāḥa a gift, on which she asked me to inform you, Messenger of Allāh (صَلَّى اللَّهُ عَلَيْهِ وَسَلَّمَ)!" He (the Messenger of Allāh) said; "Did you give the rest of your children something like this?" He replied; "No". He (صَلَّى اللَّهُ عَلَيْهِ وَسَلَّمَ) said; "Fear Allāh, and treat your children equally." He said, so he returned and took back his gift."

This is why, when Ya'qūb's (عَلَيْهِ ٱلسَّلَامُ) intense love for Yūsuf (عَلَيْهِ ٱلسَّلَامُ) became obvious to his brothers, coupled with his inability to be away from him and his preoccupation with him rather than them, they devised an evil plot – to separate him from his father (عَلَيْهِ ٱلسَّلَامُ), saying:

﴿ لَيُوسُفُ وَأَخُوهُ أَحَبُّ إِلَىٰٓ أَبِينَا مِنَّا وَنَحْنُ عُصْبَةٌ إِنَّ أَبَانَا لَفِى ضَلَـٰلٍ مُّبِينٍ ﴿٨﴾ ٱقْتُلُوا۟
يُوسُفَ أَوِ ٱطْرَحُوهُ أَرْضًا يَخْلُ لَكُمْ وَجْهُ أَبِيكُمْ وَتَكُونُوا۟ مِنۢ بَعْدِهِۦ قَوْمًا صَـٰلِحِينَ ﴿٩﴾ ﴾

"Truly, Yūsuf (Joseph) and his brother (Benjamin) are loved more by our father than we, but we are 'Usbah (a strong group). Really, our father is in a plain error. We will kill Yūsuf (Joseph) or cast him out to some (other) land, so that the favour of your father may be given to you alone, and after that you will be righteous folk (by intending repentance before committing the sin)."

[*Sūrah Yūsuf* 12:8-9]

This is a very clear statement from them that the motivation behind what they did to Yusuf (عَلَيْهِ ٱلسَّلَامُ), in separating him from his father, was being singled out for [his father's] affection. This is contrary to what many commentators of the Qur'ān mention – that Yūsuf (عَلَيْهِ ٱلسَّلَامُ) told them about his dream and they envied him for it – because this contradicts the noble verse and is tantamount to having a poor opinion of Yūsuf (عَلَيْهِ ٱلسَّلَامُ), since his father (عَلَيْهِ ٱلسَّلَامُ) asked him to hide it when he said,

﴿ قَالَ يَـٰبُنَىَّ لَا تَقْصُصْ رُءْيَاكَ عَلَىٰٓ إِخْوَتِكَ فَيَكِيدُوا۟ لَكَ كَيْدًا ۖ إِنَّ ٱلشَّيْطَـٰنَ لِلْإِنسَـٰنِ عَدُوٌّ
مُّبِينٌ ﴿٥﴾ ﴾

He (the father) said: "O' my son! Relate not your vision to your brothers, lest they arrange a plot against you. Verily! Shaitān (Satan) is to man an open enemy!

[*Sūrah Yūsuf* 12:5]

While Yūsuf (عَلَيْهِ ٱلسَّلَامُ) is better than that and knows better than to inform them of it. Nevertheless, many Biblical accounts are made popular amongst many people, even though the slightest contemplation of Islamic texts would show them the falsehood in them.

The point is that, the thing that motivated Yūsuf's brothers to do what they did was Ya'qūb's (عَلَيْهِ ٱلسَّلَامُ) favouritism of Yūsuf (عَلَيْهِ ٱلسَّلَامُ). Despite that being the case, this kind of abominable act is not permissible. They knew too that it was not permissible for them, but they thought to commit this horrendous crime and then repent to Allāh (تَبَارَكَ وَتَعَالَىٰ) afterwards. That is why they said,

﴿ وَتَكُونُوا۟ مِنۢ بَعْدِهِۦ قَوْمًا صَٰلِحِينَ ﴾

"Then after that you can be righteous people (by intending repentance before committing the sin)."

[*Sūrah Yūsuf* 12:9]

And this – for an individual to plunge himself into sin - is not allowed under any circumstance, even if he secretly intends to repent from it afterwards, because it is obligatory to stay away from sin, and when it does happen, repentance from it is compulsory.

Perhaps it was an instance of Allāh's wisdom and a mercy to Ya'qub that Allāh (تَبَارَكَ وَتَعَالَىٰ), for the sake of elevating his status in this life and the hereafter, decreed the separation that proved to be such a great source of grief and calamity for him. A further reason could be for the blessing of their reunion to have the greatest impact and be a cause for showing Allāh (تَبَارَكَ وَتَعَالَىٰ) the utmost appreciation and admiration, and so that his son, Yūsuf (عَلَيْهِ ٱلسَّلَامُ), could achieve all the honourable positions that he achieved.

﴿وَعَسَىٰٓ أَن تَكۡرَهُواْ شَيۡـٔٗا وَهُوَ خَيۡرٞ لَّكُمۡۖ وَعَسَىٰٓ أَن تُحِبُّواْ شَيۡـٔٗا وَهُوَ شَرّٞ لَّكُمۡۚ وَٱللَّهُ يَعۡلَمُ وَأَنتُمۡ لَا تَعۡلَمُونَ﴾

"And you may hate something while it is better for you; and Allāh knows, while you do not know."

[*Sūrah al-Baqarah* 2:216]

Being Cautious of the Things that may Harm Us

In this story, we are also encouraged to be wary of the things that we fear may hurt us, as may be from His (سُبْحَانَهُ وَتَعَالَىٰ) statement:

﴿قَالَ يَٰبُنَيَّ لَا تَقْصُصْ رُءْيَاكَ عَلَىٰٓ إِخْوَتِكَ فَيَكِيدُوا۟ لَكَ كَيْدًا ۖ إِنَّ ٱلشَّيْطَٰنَ لِلْإِنسَٰنِ عَدُوٌّ مُّبِينٌ ۝٥﴾

"My dear son, do not narrate your dream to your brothers, so that they do not devise a great plot against you."

[*Sūrah Yūsuf* 12:5]

Adding to that is his insistence that they must protect him when he let him go with them. Then, afterwards, when he sent his brother Benyāmīn (Benjamin) with them, he made them take oaths to the same effect. Every individual has been ordered to be cautious; if it benefits him, all is well, and if not, at least he will have no regrets.

Observing All Angles and Possibilities when Planning to do Something

Another lesson this story teaches is that part of being prudent is that when a person wishes to do something, he ought to look at it from all angles and calculate all possibilities.

Moreover, there is nothing wrong with being cautious due to a suspicion he cannot eliminate. In fact, he should be cautious of any possibility from which he fears harm, even if that means having suspicion of another person, if there are pieces of evidence that support it and necessitate it[2], like the ones mentioned in this verse[3], and like there was strong evidence for his statement:

---

[2] It is this deep understanding of this matter that should also be understood from the following words narrated from al-Ḥasan al-Baṣrī:

"Guard yourselves from the people using walls of suspicion."

Ibn Ṣa'd cited it in *aṭ-Ṭabaqāt* (2/177) with an authentic chain of narration. However, it has not been authenticated up to the Prophet. See al-Albānī in *ad-Ḍha'eefah* (1/187).

[3] **[TN]**: This is in reference to the previous verse (12:5) of *Sūrah* Yūsuf.

﴿ فَلَمَّا رَجَعُوٓا۟ إِلَىٰٓ أَبِيهِمْ قَالُوا۟ يَـٰٓأَبَانَا مُنِعَ مِنَّا ٱلْكَيْلُ فَأَرْسِلْ مَعَنَآ أَخَانَا نَكْتَلْ
وَإِنَّا لَهُۥ لَحَـٰفِظُونَ ﴿٦٣﴾ ﴾

"So, when they returned to their father, they said: "O' our father! No more measure of grain shall we get (unless we take our brother). So send our brother with us, and we shall get our measure and truly we will guard him."

[*Sūrah Yūsuf* 12:63]

Considering the fact that they had a well-known history regarding his brother, no one can blame Ya'qūb (عَلَيْهِ ٱلسَّلَامُ) for being suspicious of them like this, even though they had not neglected the youngest brother nor oppressed him.

Abstaining and Staying Away from Sins

Another moral of this story is that one must be guarded against committing sins, especially sins that lead to other sins so that they end up forming a vicious cycle. An example of this kind of sin is what Yūsuf's brothers did to him. For truly, that same one act of theirs involved many different crimes:

- Against Allāh (تَبَارَكَ وَتَعَالَى);
- Against his (Yūsuf's) parents and relatives;
- And against Yūsuf (عَلَيْهِ السَّلَامُ).

Then their lies piled up – every time there was a mention of Yūsuf (عَلَيْهِ السَّلَامُ), they told this heinous lie, which is why, when they repented, they humbled themselves and asked their dad for pardon:

﴿ قَالُواْ يَٰٓأَبَانَا ٱسْتَغْفِرْ لَنَا ذُنُوبَنَآ إِنَّا كُنَّا خَٰطِـِٔينَ ﴾

“They said, father! Ask forgiveness (from Allāh) for our sins, indeed we have been sinners.”

[*Sūrah Yūsuf* 12:97]

Some Evil Deeds are Less Contemptible than Others

Another moral of this story is that some evils are less contemptible than other evils. For instance, when they agreed to separate Yūsuf (عَلَيْهِ السَّلَامُ) from his father, and most of them were of the opinion that murder would achieve permanent detachment,

﴿ قَالَ قَآئِلٌ مِّنْهُمْ لَا تَقْتُلُواْ يُوسُفَ وَأَلْقُوهُ فِي غَيَٰبَتِ ٱلْجُبِّ يَلْتَقِطْهُ بَعْضُ ٱلسَّيَّارَةِ إِن
كُنتُمْ فَٰعِلِينَ ﴿١٠﴾ ﴾

"One from among them said: "Kill not Yūsuf (Joseph), but if you must do something, throw him down to the bottom of a well, he will be picked up by some caravan of travellers."

[*Sūrah Yūsuf* 12:10]

With that, he lightened their burden of evil.

That is why, when the caravan arrived at the water, and their water-drawer let down his bucket to get water, he rejoiced at finding Yūsuf (عَلَيْهِ ٱلسَّلَامُ) and said:

﴿ هَٰذَا غُلَٰمٌ ﴾

“There is a boy here!”

[*Sūrah Yūsuf* 12:19]

His brothers were there too, so they said, ‘In fact, he is a runaway servant boy of ours,’ then they traded with them –

﴿ وَشَرَوْهُ بِثَمَنٍۭ بَخْسٍ دَرَٰهِمَ مَعْدُودَةٍ وَكَانُوا۟ فِيهِ مِنَ ٱلزَّٰهِدِينَ ﴿٢٠﴾ ﴾

“And they sold him for a low price, - for a few Dirhams (i.e. for a few silver coins). And they were of those who regarded him insignificant.”

[*Sūrah Yūsuf* 12:20]

All they really wanted was to send him away, and stress to his buyer that he had to guard him closely so that he would not flee.

It was due to Allāh’s kindness that the one who bought him sold him in Egypt to its Azīz (the king’s vicegerent), who, when he saw him, liked him and really wanted him. He said to his wife:

﴿ أَكْرِمِى مَثْوَىٰهُ عَسَىٰٓ أَن يَنفَعَنَآ أَوْ نَتَّخِذَهُۥ وَلَدًا ﴾

“Make his stay comfortable, maybe he will profit us or we shall adopt him as a son.”

[*Sūrah Yūsuf* 12:21]

And as such, he remained with them in a state of honour and he was exempted of all duties, tedious and otherwise, while living in entire devotion to good causes. That was another kindness to Yūsuf (عَلَيْهِ السَّلَامُ), and this why Allāh (تَبَارَكَ وَتَعَالَى) said:

﴿ وَكَذَٰلِكَ مَكَّنَّا لِيُوسُفَ فِي الْأَرْضِ وَلِنُعَلِّمَهُ مِن تَأْوِيلِ الْأَحَادِيثِ ﴾

"Thus did We establish Yūsuf (Joseph) in the land, that We might teach him the interpretation of events."

[*Sūrah Yūsuf* 12:21]

Hence, his free time at the place of al-Azīz was one of the factors that contributed to his ability to acquire knowledge of useful sciences, in order to create a foundation for his high status later on in this life and in the next. This is a kindness the same way his dreams were the very first kindness shown to him, and the same as when Allāh (تَبَارَكَ وَتَعَالَى) revealed to him when his brothers threw him into the well;

﴿ وَأَوْحَيْنَا إِلَيْهِ لَتُنَبِّئَنَّهُم بِأَمْرِهِمْ هَٰذَا وَهُمْ لَا يَشْعُرُونَ ١٥ ﴾

"We inspired in him:" Indeed, you shall (one day) inform them of this their affair, when they know (you) not."

[*Sūrah Yūsuf* 12:15]

These were glad tidings for him of being saved from the situation he was in at the time, and that he would come to inform them of their doings at a time when they would be unsuspecting. This actually happened, according to His (تَبَارَكَ وَتَعَالَى) statement -

﴿ هَلۡ عَلِمۡتُم مَّا فَعَلۡتُم بِيُوسُفَ وَأَخِيهِ إِذۡ أَنتُمۡ جَٰهِلُونَ ٨٩ ﴾

"Do you know what you did with Yūsuf (Joseph) and his brother, when you were ignorant?"

[*Sūrah Yūsuf* 12:89]

The verse continues.

One cannot even begin to fathom [all] the kindnesses of the Lord and Protector.

Judging People According to their Last Deeds

One moral this story teaches us is that the crucial thing to consider concerning the condition of an individual is its positive ending, and not its disappointing beginning. The evidence for this is the fact that Yūsuf's brothers committed all the crimes that they did, however, in the end they repented to Allāh (تَبَارَكَ وَتَعَالَىٰ), sought their brother Yūsuf's, pardon and asked their parents to ask for forgiveness [from Allāh] on their behalf. As a result, they received total pardon and complete absolution. In this way, Allāh (تَبَارَكَ وَتَعَالَىٰ) overlooked their sins and guided them to the ideal condition that befitted them.

It is said that Allāh (تَبَارَكَ وَتَعَالَىٰ) made them prophets, as a number of commentators on the Qur'ān have mentioned regarding the meaning of '*al-Asbāṭ*' [the tribes] – that they are Yūsuf's twelve brothers[4].

[4] al-Alūsī said: "Most of the predecessors and those who came later are of the opinion that they were not prophets at all. As for the predecessors, it has not been relayed that any of the companions of the Prophet amongst them alleged their prophethood. Neither has it been gathered from any of their students. As for the students of the students of the companions, however, it has been relayed that Ibn Zayd

Others say that, actually, they [*al-Asbāṭ*] were a nation of righteous people. This seems to be the apparent case, since what is meant by '*al-Asbāṭ*' are the tribes of the children of Israel, and it is a general name for all the tribes that descended from the twelve sons of Ya'qūb (عَلَيْهِ السَّلَامُ), for they are the fathers of the tribes as well as members of the tribes.

This is why in Yūsuf's (عَلَيْهِ السَّلَامُ) dream he saw them as the equivalent of stars in their brightness and elevation, and this is the description of the people who posses knowledge and faith; and Allāh (تَبَارَكَ وَتَعَالَى) knows best. This is why the sun, moon and stars in dreams are interpreted as scholars and righteous people. Occasionally, they are also interpreted as kings, and the analogy is easy to see.

---

alleged their prophethood, and a small band of people agreed with him. As far as the people who came later on are concerned, the commentators are divided in opinion. Some of them, such as al-Baghawī, are of the same opinion as Ibn Zayd. While some of them, such as Ibn Kathīr and al-Qurṭūbī, went to great lengths in disproving it. Some of them, such as Ibn al-Jaūzī, quote both opinions without stating a preference for either one. Others, such as Abū Layth as-Samarqundī and al-Waḥidī, do not address the issue but allude to the invalidity of their being prophets, such as his interpreting the term "*Asbāṭ*" to mean those who were chosen for prophethood from the Children of Israel and the "ones given revelation" to mean the prophets who were given revelation. Another group mentions none of these opinions but explains the term "*Asbāṭ*" to mean Ya'qūb's sons, resulting in some people assuming this to be an assertion of their prophethood. However, this is not an explicit assertion, for the possibility that by 'sons' he may have intended his children borne by his own pair of sons. The shaykh, Ibn Taimiyyah mentions in a written work of his that deals specifically with this discussion what can be summarised as follows: "The Qur'ān, the language and contemplation all lead to the conclusion that Yūsuf (عَلَيْهِ السَّلَامُ) brothers are not prophets. There is no information in the Qur'ān, nor has been cited from the Prophet (صَلَّى ٱللَّهُ عَلَيْهِ وَسَلَّمَ) or any of his companions (رَضِيَ ٱللَّهُ عَنْهُمْ) that indicates that Allāh (تَبَارَكَ وَتَعَالَى) sent them as prophets..." See al-Alūsī, Maḥmūd in *Rūḥ al-Ma'ānī fī tafsīr al-Qur'ān al-'aẓīm wa-al-sab' al-Mathānī* (12/184).

Necessary and Voluntary Patience

Another crucial point within this story is Yūsuf's (عَلَيْهِ السَّلَامُ) achievement of the highest levels of endurance[5], namely:

Involuntary endurance: that was his endurance in the face of

[5] Ibn al-Qayyim said: "There are two kinds of endurances - physical and psychological. Each one of these is further divided into two types: voluntary and involuntary. With this, we have four categories. Firstly: the voluntary physical type, such as engaging in physically-tasking duties intentionally and voluntarily. Secondly: the involuntary physical type, such as enduring the pain from beatings, wounds, the heat and the cold, and so on. Thirdly: the voluntary psychological type, such as repressing the inner urge to do an action unacceptable by the standards of law or logic. Fourthly: the involuntary psychological type, such as being forced emotionally to endure in the face of separation from a loved one. Once you have understood these types, you should know that they are specific to the human being and are not applicable to animals except for two. These are the involuntary physical and psychological endurances, in which animals may sometimes be even stronger than human beings. Only the two voluntary types of endurance set the human being apart from the rest of the animals. Many a person's ability to endure lies in the type he shares with animals rather than the type specific to the human being, so that he is considered to be patient when in fact he is not...' See Ibn al-Qayyim in *'Uddāt aṣ-Ṣābirīn wa Dhākirāt ash-Shakirīn* (p.13-14).

his brothers' mistreatment and the separation between him and his parents that happened as a result, as well as his enduring prison for a number of years.

Voluntary endurance: [that was] his self-restraint in resisting the advances of his mistress, al-Azīz's wife. He did this, despite the strong temptations of her beauty, her high status and the fact that she was the one who tried to seduce him, locking all the doors in the process, while he was in the prime of youth and he had no one around who was related to him or who knew him originally. Despite all these things, including the force of desire, true faith and total sincerity prevented him from falling into taboo.

This is what is meant by His (سُبْحَانَهُ وَتَعَالَىٰ) statement:

﴿لَوْلَآ أَن رَّءَا بُرْهَـٰنَ رَبِّهِۦ﴾

"Had he not seen the evidence of his Lord."

[*Sūrah Yūsuf* 12:24]

That is the sign that instils the kind of belief that subdues all innate desires.

For this reason, he is at the forefront of the seven whom Allāh (تَبَارَكَ وَتَعَالَىٰ) will shelter in His shade on the day when there will be no shade except His shade, being a man who was tempted by a woman of status and beauty, but said: 'Indeed, I fear Allāh.' Then she repeatedly tried to seduce him, and sought the assistance of the women who sliced up their hands[6], but he would not be persuaded. He adhered to

---

6 **[TN]**: This is referring to the women whom the wife of al-Azīz invited to see Yūsuf's (عَلَيْهِ السَّلَامُ) beauty for themselves. Prior to that, they had mocked her for

his faith through every situation, to such an extent that he said, after she threatened him with the words:

﴿ وَلَئِن لَّمْ يَفْعَلْ مَآ ءَامُرُهُۥ لَيُسْجَنَنَّ وَلَيَكُونًا مِّنَ ٱلصَّٰغِرِينَ ﴿٣٢﴾ قَالَ رَبِّ ٱلسِّجْنُ أَحَبُّ إِلَىَّ مِمَّا يَدْعُونَنِىٓ إِلَيْهِ ﴾

"But he refused. And now if he refuses to obey my order, he shall certainly be cast into prison, and will be one of those who are disgraced. He said: "O' my Lord! Prison is more to my liking than that to which they invite me."

[*Sūrah Yūsuf* 12:32-33]

Thus, he chose prison over falling into taboo[7]. And although, he had strong endurance, he did not depend entirely on himself, but rather, he beseeched his Lord to avert from him their evil. His Lord immediately

---

seducing her boy-servant – Yūsuf. Consequently, they ended up cutting up their hands in a state of hypnosis from the extent of his beauty. See *Sūrah* Yūsuf (12:31).

[7] **[TN]**: Ibn al-Qayyim said; under the 27th Chapter: one abandons his beloved in order to avoid forbidden relations and then his beloved is made permissible for him (i.e. via a marriage contract) or Allāh (تَبَارَكَ وَتَعَالَىٰ) replaces her for him with someone better. This is based upon the principle: "Whoever leaves something for the sake of Allāh (تَبَارَكَ وَتَعَالَىٰ), Allāh (تَبَارَكَ وَتَعَالَىٰ) will compensate him with something better" just as it was the case with Yūsuf (عَلَيْهِ ٱلسَّلَامُ) who left the wife of al-Azīz's for the sake of Allāh, and chose prison over illicit actions. As a result, Allāh compensated him by giving him supremacy in the land to take whatever he wanted, and a young woman approached him seeking a permissible relationship with him, so he married her and when he came upon her, he said: "This is better than what you wanted." So contemplate over about how Allāh rewarded him for the hardship of prison and gave him supremacy in the land to take whatever he desired, debased for him the wife of al-Azīz, and she and the other women attested to his innocence. This is the *sunnah* of Allāh (تَبَارَكَ وَتَعَالَىٰ) towards His slaves - past and present until the Day of Resurrection." See Ibn al-Qayyim in *Rāwḍat al-Mūhibbīn* (1/445).

answered him and averted from him their [evil] scheme. No doubt, He (تَبَارَكَ وَتَعَالَى) is the All-Hearing, All-Seeing.

Just as he achieved all the highest levels endurance, he also achieved the furthermost levels of justice and benevolence towards the citizens when he took charge of the treasuries of the Egyptian nations. He also achieved the highest levels of generosity and lenience when he spoke to his brothers.

﴿ قَالُوا۟ تَٱللَّهِ لَقَدْ ءَاثَرَكَ ٱللَّهُ عَلَيْنَا وَإِن كُنَّا لَخَـٰطِـِٔينَ ﴿٩١﴾ قَالَ لَا تَثْرِيبَ عَلَيْكُمُ ٱلْيَوْمَ ۖ يَغْفِرُ ٱللَّهُ لَكُمْ ۖ وَهُوَ أَرْحَمُ ٱلرَّٰحِمِينَ ﴿٩٢﴾ ﴾

"They said: "By Allāh! Indeed Allāh has preferred you above us, and we certainly have been sinners." He said: "There is no reproach on you this day, may Allāh forgive you, and He is the Most Merciful of those who show mercy!."

[*Sūrah Yūsuf* 91-92]

So he climbed to the highest degrees of honour, virtue, honesty and excellence, and Allāh (تَبَارَكَ وَتَعَالَى) made the whole world sing his praise.

Sincerity

Another conclusion we can reach by looking at Yūsuf's (عَلَيْهِ السَّلَامُ) story is that devotion to Allāh (تَبَارَكَ وَتَعَالَىٰ) alone is the greatest reason for obtaining every blessing and avoiding every evil.

As Allāh (تَبَارَكَ وَتَعَالَىٰ) said:

﴿ وَلَقَدْ هَمَّتْ بِهِۦ ۖ وَهَمَّ بِهَا لَوْلَآ أَن رَّءَا بُرْهَـٰنَ رَبِّهِۦ ۚ كَذَٰلِكَ لِنَصْرِفَ عَنْهُ ٱلسُّوٓءَ
وَٱلْفَحْشَآءَ ۚ إِنَّهُۥ مِنْ عِبَادِنَا ٱلْمُخْلَصِينَ ﴿٢٤﴾ ﴾

"And indeed she did desire him and he would have inclined to her desire, had he not seen the evidence of his Lord. Thus it was, that We might turn away from him evil and illegal sexual intercourse. Surely, he was one of Our chosen, guided slaves."

[*Sūrah Yūsuf* 12:24]

In another recitation it reads "***devout***" instead of "***chosen***,"

That is, he was one of the ones whom Allāh (تَبَارَكَ وَتَعَالَى) selected specifically for the remembrance[8] of the home [of the hereafter], and the two (being devout and being chosen) are inseparable. Hence, he chose them because of their sincere devotion to Him alone; so whoever is entirely devoted to Allāh alone, Allāh (تَبَارَكَ وَتَعَالَى) will chose him and deliver him from every evil, and protect him from sinful and obscene conduct.

---

[8] [**TN**]: Commentators on the Qur'ān mention that "chosen for the remembrance of the home of the hereafter" here means that they were chosen to work for it alone, in terms of it being their only concern and also spreading the message about it to others.

Actions Based upon Strong Evidence

Also of benefit is how the story, in many places, directs to action based upon strong evidence. One [of these places] is: when al-Azīz's wife [falsely] claimed that Yūsuf (عَلَيْهِ السَّلَامُ) tried to seduce her, and he said: '*she* tried to seduce *me*;' a witness from her family testified – that is, an arbiter from her family drew the following obvious conclusion and she already had torn Yūsuf's (عَلَيْهِ السَّلَامُ) shirt while she was trying to seduce him -

﴿إِن كَانَ قَمِيصُهُۥ قُدَّ مِن قُبُلٍ فَصَدَقَتْ وَهُوَ مِنَ ٱلْكَٰذِبِينَ ﴿٢٦﴾﴾

"If it be that his shirt is torn from the front, then her tale is true and he is a liar."

[*Sūrah Yūsuf* 12:26]

Because it proves he approached her and that he was the one who initiated the seduction –

﴿وَإِن كَانَ قَمِيصُهُۥ قُدَّ مِن دُبُرٍ فَكَذَبَتْ وَهُوَ مِنَ ٱلصَّٰدِقِينَ ﴿٢٧﴾﴾

"But if it be that his shirt is torn from the back, then she has told a lie and he is speaking the truth."

[*Sūrah Yūsuf* 12:27]

That is exactly what happened, because she wanted him and he was running away from her, so she ripped his shirt from behind. With that, it became clear to them that she was the seductress in that particular situation. Later on, she made a total confession when she said,

﴿ ٱلْـَٔـٰنَ حَصْحَصَ ٱلْحَقُّ أَنَا۠ رَٰوَدتُّهُۥ عَن نَّفْسِهِۦ وَإِنَّهُۥ لَمِنَ ٱلصَّـٰدِقِينَ ﴿٥١﴾ ذَٰلِكَ لِيَعْلَمَ أَنِّى لَمْ أَخُنْهُ بِٱلْغَيْبِ وَأَنَّ ٱللَّهَ لَا يَهْدِى كَيْدَ ٱلْخَآئِنِينَ ﴿٥٢﴾ ﴾

"Now the truth has come to light – I was the one who tried to seduce him, and indeed he is a truthful man. [Then Yūsuf (Joseph) said: "I asked for this enquiry] in order that he (al-'Azīz) may know that I betrayed him not in secret.."[9]

[*Sūrah Yūsuf* 12:51-52]

Another instance of action based on evidence was at the discovery of the king's cup in his brother's baggage, and their judgment of him according to the laws of theft due to this strong evidence.

---

[9] Ibn al-Qayyim said; "Working with the evidence is necessary by law, logic and convention." See Ibn al-Qaayim in *Ighāthat al-Lahfān min-Maṣāyid al-Shayṭān* (2/66) and *Badā i'ul Fawā iḍ* (4/820).

The Obligation of Avoiding Sources of Temptation

Another moral this story teaches is that a slave of Allāh should avoid sources of temptation – the way Yūsuf (عَلَيْهِ السَّلَامُ) did when al-'Azīz's wife tried to seduce him.

Now, you should know that many commentators on the Qur'ān mentioned, regarding the nature of the sign that Yūsuf (عَلَيْهِ السَّلَامُ) saw at the moment he refrained from committing the obscenity, Biblical accounts that contradict both common sense and the religion [of Islām], as well as contradict the state of perfection of the prophets[10].

[10] The Great Learned Man, Muḥammad al-Amīn al-Shinqīṭī said after having quoted some of the statements of the learned community on this topic, "These opinions that I saw being attributed to these scholars are of two kinds. One that cannot be verified through a sound authority up to the person quoted. The unacceptability of this one poses no dilemma. The other kind is that which has been verified to be from some of those mentioned through a sound authority. It is almost certain that those of them from which this opinion has been confirmed got it from none other than Jewish traditions, since there is no room for conjecture here and none of it has been attributed to the Prophet." al-Shinqīṭī, Muḥammad al-Amīn in *Aḍwā' al-Bayān Fī īḍāḥ al-Qur'ān bi al-Qur'ān* (3/60).

To this effect, some of them said that Jibrīl (عَلَيْهِ ٱلسَّلَامُ) appeared to him in the air; or that Ya'qūb (عَلَيْهِ ٱلسَّلَامُ) appeared to him while biting on his thumb, or such similar events, the likes of which if they happened would deter the most erroneous of people from committing a crime, and for which reason, all of them are false.

Other false opinions include what some of them said regarding His (تَبَارَكَ وَتَعَالَىٰ) statement;

﴿ وَلَقَدْ هَمَّتْ بِهِۦ وَهَمَّ بِهَا ﴾

> **"And she had indeed desired him and he would have inclined to her desire."**
>
> [*Sūrah Yūsuf* 12:24]

That it means he intended to beat her – and this is a clear perversion [of the apparent meaning]. The intention of the owner of this opinion was to evade the commonly known meaning of 'desire' for fear that it would allude to some deficiency [in Yūsuf]. However, this opinion is in danger of being a belittlement of the prophets, for indeed, when a slave resists his desires, lusts and so on, and chooses to fear [Allāh] and have faith, he is displaying a characteristic of perfection. As Allāh (تَبَارَكَ وَتَعَالَىٰ) says,

﴿ وَلِمَنْ خَافَ مَقَامَ رَبِّهِۦ جَنَّتَانِ ﴿٤٦﴾ ﴾

> **"However, for him who fears the standing [for judgment] before his Lord, there will be two Gardens (i.e. in Paradise)."**
>
> [*Sūrah ar-Raḥmān* 55:46]

Moreover, it has been confirmed to be true in the authentic reports from the Prophet that he said,

> "Whoever decides to commit a sin but does not [end up] doing it, Allāh will write one good deed for him – [saying] he only left it because of Me."[11]

i.e. his leaving it for the sake of Allah (تَبَارَكَ وَتَعَالَىٰ), fearing His Punishment and anticipating His (تَبَارَكَ وَتَعَالَىٰ) Reward - is one of the greatest acts of worship; and Allah knows best.

---

[11] See al-Bukhārī (no.7501) and Muslim (no.129), on the authority of Ibn Abbās (رَضِيَ ٱللَّهُ عَنْهُ). This is Muslim's wording.

The Extent of Yūsuf's Beauty

One may also gather from this story the extent of Yūsuf's physical beauty, may Allāh (تَبَارَكَ وَتَعَالَىٰ) raise his repute, which stole the heart of al-Azīz's wife and infatuated her.

In addition, when the women saw him they cut their hands and praised him,

﴿ وَقُلْنَ حَٰشَ لِلَّهِ مَا هَٰذَا بَشَرًا إِنْ هَٰذَآ إِلَّا مَلَكٌ كَرِيمٌ ﴾

"How perfect is Allāh (or Allāh forbid)! No man is this! This is none other than a noble angel!"

[*Sūrah Yūsuf* 12:31]

It also shows us the greatness of his inner beauty, which was a combination of modesty, complete sincerity, and self-control.

The Obligation of Retreating to Allāh

Another moral that may be extracted from this story is that it is incumbent upon an individual to retreat to Allāh (تَبَارَكَ وَتَعَالَى) when he fears that he might fall into the ordeal of disobedience and sin. Along with that he must practise self-restraint and make a great effort to avoid the sin - the way Yūsuf (عَلَيْهِ السَّلَامُ) did when he called on his Lord saying,

﴿ وَإِلَّا تَصْرِفْ عَنِّي كَيْدَهُنَّ أَصْبُ إِلَيْهِنَّ وَأَكُن مِّنَ الْجَاهِلِينَ ﴾

"Unless You turn away their plot from me, I will feel inclined towards them and be one (of those who commit sin and deserve blame or those who do deeds) of the ignorant."

[*Sūrah Yūsuf* 12:33]

The truth is that the individual has no power, strength, or protection (from sins and other harmful things) except through Allāh's help

(تَبَارَكَ وَتَعَالَىٰ). The individual has been ordered to perform obligations, leave the prohibited, and be patient with the decree of Allāh (تَبَارَكَ وَتَعَالَىٰ), as well as to seek aid from [Allāh (تَبَارَكَ وَتَعَالَىٰ)] the King, the Most Appreciative.

The Virtue of Complete Faith, Certainty, Confidence and Remembrance

Another useful point learnt from Yūsuf's story is the virtue of complete faith, certainty and finding reassurance in Allāh (تَبَارَكَ وَتَعَالَىٰ) and His remembrance. Yūsuf (عَلَيْهِ ٱلسَّلَامُ) demonstrated this when he (عَلَيْهِ ٱلسَّلَامُ) took on these characteristics and they, as a result, guaranteed his stability in all his affairs and in working on the assignments of his current job while in every circumstance and in all his comings and goings, his mind was tranquil, and his soul, resolute. He felt no agitation as a result of the distance between him, his father and loved ones, despite his appreciation of the deep longing and utmost affection that existed between him and his parents, and especially between him and his father, Ya'qūb (عَلَيْهِ ٱلسَّلَامُ). He, moreover, knew where his father was and he had the ability to contact him, but Allāh's (تَبَارَكَ وَتَعَالَىٰ) wisdom necessitated that they would not meet except under those extreme and severely difficult circumstances mentioned earlier.

Allāh (تَبَارَكَ وَتَعَالَىٰ) helped him and strengthened him with His support, and this is one of the most significant rewards of having faith.

The Permissibility of Seeking Help from Mankind in Regular Tasks

This story also teaches that it is permissible to ask someone besides Allāh for help in regular tasks that he is able to perform[12] - by acting, speaking or relaying information. For example, when Yūsuf (عَلَيْهِ السَّلَامُ) said to the one he knew would be freed out of the two prisoners,

﴿ٱذۡكُرۡنِي عِندَ رَبِّكَ﴾

"Mention me to your master."

[*Sūrah Yūsuf* 12:42]

---

12 [**TN**] If it is the case that you must seek help from people in a permissible matter, firstly turn to Allāh and seek His help before you turn to the creation of Allāh. If you turn to the creation of Allāh, then it must be from someone who has three attributes; 1) They must be alive, 2) They must have the ability to help you, and 3) They must be present. Refer to *Sharḥ Kitāb at-Tawḥīd* by Shaykh Ṣāliḥ al-Fawzān (p.276).

The fact that Yūsuf (عَلَيْهِ ٱلسَّلَامُ) did not scold this man to whom he entrusted the duty of mentioning him to his master – and who then forgot – shows the purity of Yūsuf's (عَلَيْهِ ٱلسَّلَامُ) purpose[13] and his excellent character. He came to him to ask him about the king's dream and he answered him without scolding him, being harsh to him or treating him rudely. It is by the virtue of his good qualities that an individual may live a good life in the current reality and in the reality to come.

---

13 **[TN]**: He is only concerned with pleasing Allāh (تَبَارَكَ وَتَعَالَىٰ) and helping His creation to succeed in this life and the hereafter, which is why he asked for nothing in return for his interpretation of the dream even though he was in need. Nor was he upset at the man for not "returning" the previous favour, since he did it to gain only Allāh's (تَبَارَكَ وَتَعَالَىٰ) favour.

Clarifying Accusations

Another benefit found in this story is that when a person is accused of something he is innocent of, he should not be condemned for seeking the ways and means that will prove his innocence and make it clear to the people.

Just as Yūsuf (عَلَيْهِ السَّلَامُ) did. Despite his lengthy stay in confinement, when the messenger came to call him to present himself to the king, he said,

﴿ ٱرْجِعْ إِلَىٰ رَبِّكَ فَسْـَٔلْهُ مَا بَالُ ٱلنِّسْوَةِ ٱلَّـٰتِى قَطَّعْنَ أَيْدِيَهُنَّ ۚ ﴿٥٠﴾ ﴾

"Return to your master and ask him what happened with the women who cut their hands..."

[*Sūrah Yūsuf* 12:50]

And so on until the end of the verse, to the effect that his total and undeniable innocence became clear to everyone. The result was that he did not leave prison to meet the king except in a state of being vindicated, [and in a state of] respect and prestige and while they were in awe of his knowledge, superiority and his integrity, may Allāh (تَبَارَكَ وَتَعَالَىٰ) raise his repute and save him from all deficiency.

Interpretation of Dreams and Advice

We also learn from this story that Yūsuf (عَلَيْهِ السَّلَامُ) combined between interpreting the dream, and offering them advice on what they should do and arrange during the years of fertility in preparation for the years of infertility. The king said to him at the time:

﴿ إِنَّكَ ٱلْيَوْمَ لَدَيْنَا مَكِينٌ أَمِينٌ ﴾

"As of today, you are to us considered a man of authority and trust."

[*Sūrah Yūsuf* 12:54]

That is, you have authority over the affairs of the kingdom and their management. He was entrusted with all the affairs of the kingdom due to his trustworthiness, capability and reliability.

The king himself, therefore, was the one who originally gave him authority and entrusted to him the affairs of the kingdom. Yūsuf (عَلَيْهِ ٱلسَّلَامُ) was then the one who suggested that he should be specifically in charge of the land's stores and treasury, and also its taxes and its expenditure for public benefit, which is why he said,

﴿ قَالَ ٱجْعَلْنِي عَلَىٰ خَزَآئِنِ ٱلْأَرْضِ إِنِّي حَفِيظٌ عَلِيمٌ ﴿٥٥﴾ ﴾

"Place me in charge of the land's treasuries; I will indeed guard them with full knowledge (as a minister of finance in Egypt, in place of al-'Azīz who was dead at that time)."

[*Sūrah Yūsuf* 12:55]

That is, I will take good care of the revenue and harvest, and I know how to spend and manage them. If you do as I request, I will focus on growing enormous amounts of crop and saving them in their stores and their ears; and I will work out the economics of the public's consumption during the years of fertility, to conserve the harvest and allow it to be enough to sustain everyone.

Following that, when the years of infertility came and famine spread throughout the Egyptian territories and its neighbouring lands, and what the people had with them ran out, they began to head for Egypt from every direction. He began to ration food for them in a fair and efficient way, according to need, never giving more than the amount a camel can carry for fear that those who did not need it would hoard it, which would in turn place the needy and those in necessity at a disadvantage. This is why part of what Yūsuf's brothers used to convince their father to send Benyāmīn with them was that they said,

﴿ وَنَزْدَادُ كَيْلَ بَعِيرٍ ﴾

"And we will gain the equivalent of a camel's load [of food]."

[*Sūrah Yūsuf* 12:65]

That is, if he were to be with us, our ration would increase by one camel load, which they needed because Ya'qūb's (عَلَيْهِ السَّلَامُ) family was large, needing a lot of provision.

These important duties, at the hands of Yūsuf (عَلَيْهِ السَّلَامُ), brought about tremendous benefits for the people. They removed necessities, satisfied needs, and eased hardships and distress.

Showing Hospitality towards Guests

The story also shows the legitimacy of showing hospitality towards [one's] guests and that it is part of the teachings of the messengers of Allāh (تَبَارَكَ وَتَعَالَىٰ) that is also endorsed by this current [Islamic] law. We learn this from Yūsuf's (عَلَيْهِ السَّلَامُ) words:

﴿ أَلَا تَرَوْنَ أَنِّي أُوفِي الْكَيْلَ وَأَنَا خَيْرُ الْمُنزِلِينَ ﴿٥٩﴾ ﴾

"Do you not see how I give the full measure [for your payment] and how I am the best of hosts?"

[*Sūrah Yūsuf* 12:59]

Protection from the Evil Eye

From this story, it may also be gathered that taking measures to gain protection against the evil eye or other harmful things is not disallowed, and is actually permissible or even recommended, depending on the situation.

This is because, even though everything is according to Allāh's (تَبَارَكَ وَتَعَالَىٰ) decision and decree, the devices used for protection against or the overcoming of harm are [also] part of Allāh's (تَبَارَكَ وَتَعَالَىٰ) decision and decree. However, there is the condition that the individual uses them while he is fully dependant on the one who brought them about. Ya'qūb (عَلَيْهِ السَّلَامُ) demonstrated this when he was about to advise his children, when he was sending Benyāmīn with them, saying,

﴿ وَقَالَ يَٰبَنِيَّ لَا تَدۡخُلُواْ مِنۢ بَابٖ وَٰحِدٖ وَٱدۡخُلُواْ مِنۡ أَبۡوَٰبٖ مُّتَفَرِّقَةٖۖ وَمَآ أُغۡنِي عَنكُم مِّنَ ٱللَّهِ مِن شَيۡءٍۖ إِنِ ٱلۡحُكۡمُ إِلَّا لِلَّهِۖ عَلَيۡهِ تَوَكَّلۡتُۖ وَعَلَيۡهِ فَلۡيَتَوَكَّلِ ٱلۡمُتَوَكِّلُونَ ٦٧ ﴾

"And he said: "O' my sons! Do not enter by one gate, but enter by different gates, and I cannot avail you against Allāh at all. Verily! The decision rests only

with Allāh. In him, I put my trust and let all those that trust, put their trust in Him."

[*Sūrah Yūsuf* 12:67]

Allāh (تَبَارَكَ وَتَعَالَى) informs us that they obeyed their father's orders, and that this order did not help them in any way except that it was an urge that Ya'qūb (عَلَيْهِ ٱلسَّلَامُ) needed to satisfy, and a father's concern for his children. The [Islāmic] law came with confirmation of the existence of religious and worldly channels of benefit, and an encouragement to make use of them whilst seeking Allāh's help (تَبَارَكَ وَتَعَالَى).

It has been cited, on good authority all the way to the Prophet (صَلَّى ٱللَّهُ عَلَيْهِ وَسَلَّمَ), that he said,

> "Work hard for the things that are good for you and seek Allāh's help."[14]

---

[14] Abū Hurairah (رَضِيَ ٱللَّهُ عَنْهُ) cited the Messenger of Allāh (صَلَّى ٱللَّهُ عَلَيْهِ وَسَلَّمَ) saying, "A strong believer is better and loved more by Allāh (تَبَارَكَ وَتَعَالَى) than a weak believer, while each one has his merits. Work hard for things that are worthwhile and ask Allāh (تَبَارَكَ وَتَعَالَى) for help. Do not give up. And If you run into difficulty, do not say, if only I had done this and that, it would have been different. Rather, just say, this is Allāh's (تَبَارَكَ وَتَعَالَى) decree and he did what he willed. Saying "if only" opens the door to the work of the devil. See Muslim (no.2664), on the authority of Abū Hurairah (رَضِيَ ٱللَّهُ عَنْهُ).

The Permissibility of using Tricks and Ruses to Obtain a Right

This story also shows the permissibility of using tricks and ruses to obtain some obligatory, recommended or permissible right, the way Yūsuf (عَلَيْهِ ٱلسَّلَامُ) did to get his brother, when he placed the cup in his brother's luggage, then an announcer called out to them after their departure:

﴿ أَيَّتُهَا ٱلْعِيرُ إِنَّكُمْ لَسَٰرِقُونَ ﴾

"You are indeed thieves, O [people of the] caravan!"

Events followed, up until where Allāh (تَبَارَكَ وَتَعَالَىٰ) says,

﴿ فَبَدَأَ بِأَوْعِيَتِهِمْ قَبْلَ وِعَآءِ أَخِيهِ ثُمَّ ٱسْتَخْرَجَهَا مِن وِعَآءِ أَخِيهِ ۚ كَذَٰلِكَ كِدْنَا لِيُوسُفَ ۖ مَا كَانَ لِيَأْخُذَ أَخَاهُ فِى دِينِ ٱلْمَلِكِ إِلَّآ أَن يَشَآءَ ٱللَّهُ ۚ نَرْفَعُ دَرَجَٰتٍ مَّن نَّشَآءُ ۗ وَفَوْقَ كُلِّ ذِى عِلْمٍ عَلِيمٌ ﴿٧٦﴾ ﴾

"So he [Yūsuf (Joseph)] began (the search) in their bags before the bag of his brother. "Then he pulled it out of his brother's container." Thus did We plan for

Yūsuf (Joseph). He could not take his brother by the law of the king (as a slave), except that Allāh willed it. (So Allāh made the brothers to bind themselves with their way of "punishment, i.e. enslaving of a thief.") We raise to degrees whom We please, but over all those endowed with knowledge is the All-Knowing (Allāh)."

[*Sūrah Yūsuf* 12:70-76]

The reason he did this to his brother was in order to make him stay with him without his other brothers knowing. When they established that he did take the cup, he asked them about the rule regarding someone who steals in their religion.

They replied,

﴿قَالُوا۟ جَزَٰٓؤُهُۥ مَن وُجِدَ فِى رَحْلِهِۦ فَهُوَ جَزَٰٓؤُهُۥ ۚ كَذَٰلِكَ نَجْزِى ٱلظَّٰلِمِينَ ﴿٧٥﴾﴾

"They [Yusuf's (Joseph) brothers] said: "The penalty should be that he, in whose bag it is found, should be held for the punishment (of the crime). Thus we punish the wrong-doers!"

[*Sūrah Yūsuf* 12:75]

That is, the thief's punishment is that he becomes the property of the person from whom he stole. Hence, they judged themselves according to this ruling, which was what Yūsuf (عَلَيْهِ السَّلَامُ) intended. Had he had judged him according to the law of the king of Egypt, it would have been a different verdict. Allāh (تَبَارَكَ وَتَعَالَى) made this exploit and this verdict possible for him so that his brother could remain with him. There is nothing wrong with this type of trick, and what is actually impermissible are the tricks and ruses used to make forbidden things permissible and to waive obligatory acts.

The Use of Misleading Words

The story also provides examples of the use of misleading words or language when necessary. Using misleading language removes the need to lie.

For instance, his statement:

﴿ قَالُوا۟ جَزَٰٓؤُهُۥ مَن وُجِدَ فِى رَحْلِهِۦ فَهُوَ جَزَٰٓؤُهُۥ ۚ كَذَٰلِكَ نَجْزِى ٱلظَّٰلِمِينَ ﴿٧٥﴾ ﴾

"They [Yusuf's (Joseph) brothers] said: "The penalty should be that he, in whose bag it is found, should be held for the punishment (of the crime). Thus we punish the wrong-doers!"

[*Sūrah Yūsuf* 12:75]

He did not say, "*He stole it.*"

Likewise is his statement:

﴿ قَالَ مَعَاذَ ٱللَّهِ أَن نَّأْخُذَ إِلَّا مَن وَجَدْنَا مَتَٰعَنَا عِندَهُۥٓ إِنَّآ إِذًا لَّظَٰلِمُونَ ﴿٧٩﴾ ﴾

"He said: "Allāh forbid, that we should take anyone but him with whom we found our property. Indeed (if we did so), we should be wrong-doers."

[*Sūrah Yūsuf* 12:79]

Rather than saying, "*The one who stole our property*."

What if a person were to say, "But this is a [false] accusation against an innocent person?"

The reply is that he only did it with the permission of his brother and his approval, and as long as there is approval, there is nothing wrong with it.

Attesting to What One Knows

Another point of benefit from this story is that it is not permissible for a person to affirm except that which he knows.

This is due their statement:

﴿ شَهِدْنَآ إِلَّا بِمَا عَلِمْنَا ﴾

> **"And we testify not except according to what we know."**
>
> [Sūrah Yūsuf 12:81]

This "*knowledge*" may be a consequence of a person's confession, and the presence of the stolen item with him, whether it is in his hand or in his luggage. This also shows that the presence of the stolen item in the hands of the thief is proof and an indicator that he is indeed the thief. This is why they judged Yūsuf's brother as a thief.

The Great Trial with which Allāh Tested His Prophet and Chosen One

Another noteworthy observation from this story is the great trial with which Allāh (تَبَارَكَ وَتَعَالَىٰ) tested His prophet and chosen one, Ya'qūb (عَلَيْهِ السَّلَامُ). Considering that He decreed the separation between him and Yūsuf (عَلَيْهِ السَّلَامُ) for such a long period, which seems most likely to have been thirty years or more. Some of that was the period that he spent in the home of the al-Azīz before his imprisonment, which was probably between seven and ten years, give or take. Then he stayed between three and nine years in prison and most are of the opinion that it was seven years.

After his exit [from prison] came the seven years of abundance and fertility. These all add up to about twenty-one years. Then there were the seven years of famine. Yūsuf's brothers came to him repeatedly during that period, and it is seems that their reunion was at the end of those seven years. These add up to approximately thirty years; and all this while, Ya'qūb's heart was full of grief. He cried endlessly until his grief made his eyes fade, and he lost his sight, while he waited patiently for Allāh's (تَبَارَكَ وَتَعَالَىٰ) resolution and looked forward to his reward with Allāh (تَبَارَكَ وَتَعَالَىٰ).

He promised himself that he would be patient and in fact, he fulfilled that promise, and his words:

﴿إِنَّمَآ أَشۡكُواْ بَثِّي وَحُزۡنِيٓ إِلَى ٱللَّهِ﴾

> **"I only complain to Allāh about my grief and sorrow."**
>
> [*Sūrah Yūsuf* 12:86]

- do not contradict this fact, because complaining to Allāh (تَبَارَكَ وَتَعَالَى) does not invalidate patience; rather, complaining to *other than* Allāh (تَبَارَكَ وَتَعَالَى) does.

After Distress Comes Relief

Another noteworthy observation from the story of Yūsuf (عَلَيْهِ ٱلسَّلَامُ) is that distress comes hand-in-hand with relief.

This observation comes from the time when Ya'qūb's (عَلَيْهِ ٱلسَّلَامُ) sorrow reached its peak and he said, 'Oh! How I grieve for Yūsuf (عَلَيْهِ ٱلسَّلَامُ)!' After which he said,

﴿ يَٰبَنِيَّ ٱذۡهَبُواْ فَتَحَسَّسُواْ مِن يُوسُفَ وَأَخِيهِ وَلَا تَاْيۡـَٔسُواْ مِن رَّوۡحِ ٱللَّهِۖ إِنَّهُۥ لَا يَاْيۡـَٔسُ
مِن رَّوۡحِ ٱللَّهِ إِلَّا ٱلۡقَوۡمُ ٱلۡكَٰفِرُونَ ٨٧ ﴾

"My children! Go and enquire about Yūsuf (Joseph) and his brother, and never give up hope of Allāh's Mercy. Certainly no one despairs of Allāh's Mercy, except the people who disbelieve."

[*Sūrah Yūsuf* 12:87]

Then when they entered upon Yūsuf (عَلَيْهِ السَّلَامُ) they presented themselves as people desperately in need, saying,

﴿ يَٰٓأَيُّهَا ٱلْعَزِيزُ مَسَّنَا وَأَهْلَنَا ٱلضُّرُّ وَجِئْنَا بِبِضَٰعَةٍ مُّزْجَىٰةٍ ﴾

"O' Azīz! A hard time has hit us and our family, and we have brought but poor capital."

[*Sūrah Yūsuf* 12:88]

That is, small and beggarly, not enough for anything –

﴿ فَأَوْفِ لَنَا ٱلْكَيْلَ وَتَصَدَّقْ عَلَيْنَآ ۖ إِنَّ ٱللَّهَ يَجْزِى ٱلْمُتَصَدِّقِينَ ﴾

"So pay us full measure and be charitable to us. Truly, Allāh does reward the charitable."

[*Sūrah Yūsuf* 12:88]

It was at that point, when the strain of their affliction had utterly reached its peak, he made himself known to them. It was the most welcoming news to his parents, his brothers and their family, and their adversity and wretchedness left them and were replaced by happiness, comfort and relief.

Allāh Tests His Prophets and Chosen Ones Using Both Difficult and Comfortable Circumstances

A major theme in the story of Yūsuf (عَلَيْهِ ٱلسَّلَامُ) is that Allāh (تَبَارَكَ وَتَعَالَىٰ) tests His prophets and chosen ones using both difficult and pleasing circumstances, as well as happiness and sorrow, and ease and hardship, so that He can extract worship from them under both circumstances - through gratitude during times of ease, and patience during times of difficulty and tribulation. This is so that they may receive His blessings in full. He tested Ya'qūb and Yūsuf (عَلَيْهِمَا ٱلسَّلَامُ) for this purpose and like them, His other prophets and chosen ones.

Informing Others of One's Feelings

The story shows the permissibility of informing others about one's feelings, an illness one has, one's state of poverty, etc, when it is not done out of bitterness. This is observable in the words of Yūsuf's brothers:

﴿ مَسَّنَا وَأَهْلَنَا ٱلضُّرُّ ﴾

"A hard time has hit us and our family."

[*Sūrah Yūsuf* 12:88]

Yūsuf (عَلَيْهِ ٱلسَّلَامُ) approved.

The Virtue of Taqwā and Patience

Another noteworthy point learnt from this story is the virtue of *taqwā* [protecting oneself against Allāh's (تَبَارَكَ وَتَعَالَىٰ) punishment by obeying Him] and patience, and that every blessing in this life and the hereafter happens as a consequence of these two things, and that the outcome for the people who are characterised by them is the best of outcomes, due to his words:

﴿قَدْ مَنَّ ٱللَّهُ عَلَيْنَآ ۖ إِنَّهُۥ مَن يَتَّقِ وَيَصْبِرْ فَإِنَّ ٱللَّهَ لَا يُضِيعُ أَجْرَ ٱلْمُحْسِنِينَ﴾

"Allāh has been gracious to us; there is no doubt that whoever has *taqwā* with obedience to Him and is patient, Allāh never fails to reward those who excel in doing good deeds."

[*Sūrah Yūsuf* 12:90]

Additionally, it is considered a proclamation of the blessings of Allāh (تَبَارَكَ وَتَعَالَىٰ) for an individual to speak about his own *taqwā* and patience, as long as it is true and [mention of them] is for a good purpose.

Allāh (تَبَارَكَ وَتَعَالَىٰ) says:

﴿ وَأَمَّا بِنِعْمَةِ رَبِّكَ فَحَدِّثْ ۝١١ ﴾

"And proclaim the blessings of your Lord."

[*Sūrah ad- Ḍuhā* 93:11]

The word "blessings" includes worldly and religious blessings. Allāh (تَبَارَكَ وَتَعَالَىٰ) gathers for the pious both the good of this life and the hereafter, as Allāh indicates in this verse and the previous one:

﴿ نُصِيبُ بِرَحْمَتِنَا مَن نَّشَآءُ ۖ وَلَا نُضِيعُ أَجْرَ ٱلْمُحْسِنِينَ ۝٥٦ وَلَأَجْرُ ٱلْءَاخِرَةِ خَيْرٌ لِّلَّذِينَ ءَامَنُوا۟ وَكَانُوا۟ يَتَّقُونَ ۝٥٧ ﴾

"We bestow of Our Mercy on whom We please, and We make not to be lost the reward of al-Muḥsinūn. And verily, the reward of the Hereafter is better for those who believe and used to fear Allāh and keep their duty to Him (by abstaining from all kinds of sins and evil deeds and by performing all kinds of righteous good deeds)."

[*Sūrah Yūsuf* 12:56-57]

Furthermore, an individual should remember the sad and difficult times during the times of happiness and ease, so that he may increase in his gratitude and appreciation of Allāh (تَبَارَكَ وَتَعَالَىٰ). This is why Yūsuf (عَلَيْهِ ٱلسَّلَامُ) said:

﴿ وَقَدْ أَحْسَنَ بِىٓ إِذْ أَخْرَجَنِى مِنَ ٱلسِّجْنِ وَجَآءَ بِكُم مِّنَ ٱلْبَدْوِ ۝١٠٠ ﴾

"He was indeed good to me, when He took me out of prison, and brought you (all here) out from the wilderness."

[*Sūrah Yūsuf* 12:100]

Begging Allāh for Steadfastness

This story shows that one should always beg Allāh (تَبَارَكَ وَتَعَالَىٰ) to strengthen his faith for him, and should also perform acts that aid him in strengthening it.

He should ask Allāh (تَبَارَكَ وَتَعَالَىٰ) for His full blessing and a favourable ending [to his life], and he should use [mention of] His Lord's current favours to him to appeal to him to crown them for him and to make his final outcome a good one. As Yūsuf (عَلَيْهِ ٱلسَّلَامُ) said,

﴿رَبِّ قَدْ ءَاتَيْتَنِى مِنَ ٱلْمُلْكِ وَعَلَّمْتَنِى مِن تَأْوِيلِ ٱلْأَحَادِيثِ ۚ فَاطِرَ ٱلسَّمَٰوَٰتِ وَٱلْأَرْضِ أَنتَ
وَلِىِّۦ فِى ٱلدُّنْيَا وَٱلْءَاخِرَةِ ۖ تَوَفَّنِى مُسْلِمًا وَأَلْحِقْنِى بِٱلصَّٰلِحِينَ ١٠١﴾

"My Lord! You have indeed bestowed on me of the sovereignty, and taught me the interpretation of dreams; The (only) Creator of the heavens and the earth! You are my Wali (Protector, Helper, Supporter, Guardian, etc.) in this world and in the Hereafter, cause me to die as a Muslim (the one submitting to Your Will), and join me with the righteous."

[*Sūrah Yūsuf* 12:101]

Contrary to what some people think, Yūsuf (عَلَيْهِ ٱلسَّلَامُ) is not wishing for death here. Rather, he is asking Allāh (سُبْحَانَهُ وَتَعَالَىٰ), like a slave should always ask his Lord, that He should make the ending to his life a good one and that He should take his life while he is practising Islām.

Yūsuf's Forgiveness through Allāh's Grace

One can see how, by Allāh's (تَبَارَكَ وَتَعَالَىٰ) grace, Yūsuf (عَلَيْهِ ٱلسَّلَامُ) was able to so generously forgive his brothers, and how he forgave them for the past, and promised that he would neither criticise them nor make any mention of it in the future, since that would hurt and sadden them, while they had already shown utter remorse [for what they did]. This is why Yūsuf (عَلَيْهِ ٱلسَّلَامُ) said:

﴿مِنۢ بَعۡدِ أَن نَّزَغَ ٱلشَّيۡطَٰنُ بَيۡنِي وَبَيۡنَ إِخۡوَتِيٓۚ﴾

"After *Shaitān* (Satan) had sown enmity between me and my brothers."

[*Sūrah Yūsuf* 12:100]

Rather than saying, "*The devil incited them.*".

Instead, he ascribed the act to the devil, the one who caused the split between him and his brothers. This is an example of outright chivalry, manliness and generosity.

The Major Testament to [the Truth of] the Message of Muḥammad

This great story contains a major testament to [the truth of] Muḥammad's Message (صَلَّى ٱللَّهُ عَلَيْهِ وَسَلَّمَ), since he narrated the story precisely – and he had never read any of the previous books [of revelation], never sat with anyone who was familiar with them, and never learnt about them from anyone. It was revelation that Allāh (تَبَارَكَ وَتَعَالَىٰ) revealed to him, nothing more, nothing less. This is why Allāh (تَبَارَكَ وَتَعَالَىٰ) said,

﴿ تِلْكَ مِنْ أَنۢبَآءِ ٱلْغَيْبِ نُوحِيهَآ إِلَيْكَ ۖ مَا كُنتَ تَعْلَمُهَآ أَنتَ وَلَا قَوْمُكَ مِن قَبْلِ هَٰذَا ۖ فَٱصْبِرْ ۖ
إِنَّ ٱلْعَٰقِبَةَ لِلْمُتَّقِينَ ﴿٤٩﴾ ﴾

"That was from amongst the stories of the unknown. We reveal it to you. Neither did you, nor your people know it before this."

[*Sūrah Ḥūd* 11:49]

Allāh (تَبَارَكَ وَتَعَالَىٰ) says this about Yūsuf's story and the stories of other prophets, and that is because there are two types of unknown. One involves past events, the knowledge of which had disappeared until Allāh (تَبَارَكَ وَتَعَالَىٰ) revealed them. The other involves future events that Allāh (تَبَارَكَ وَتَعَالَىٰ) revealed before they happened, then happened, and continue to occur gradually according the Prophet's (صَلَّىٰ ٱللَّٰهُ عَلَيْهِ وَسَلَّمَ) reports in the Qur'ān and his confirmed teachings (*Sunnah*). All of these are testaments to [the truth] of his message.

The Nature of the Self

Another point worthy of note is that in the statement of Allāh (تَبَارَكَ وَتَعَالَىٰ):

﴿ إِنَّ ٱلنَّفْسَ لَأَمَّارَةٌۢ بِٱلسُّوٓءِ إِلَّا مَا رَحِمَ رَبِّيٓۚ إِنَّ رَبِّي غَفُورٌ رَّحِيمٌ ﴿٥٣﴾ ﴾

"No doubt, the (human) self is inclined to evil, except when my Lord bestows His Mercy (upon whom He wills). Verily, my Lord is Oft-Forgiving, Most Merciful."

[*Sūrah Yūsuf* 12:53]

There is proof that this is the inherent nature of the self, and that it cannot be free of this nature except through Allāh's (تَبَارَكَ وَتَعَالَىٰ) care and mercy. This is because the self is ignorant and corrupt, and ignorance and corruption breed nothing but evil.

If Allāh (تَبَارَكَ وَتَعَالَىٰ) is merciful to a slave and is kind to him by giving him practical knowledge and giving him an honest approach in his behaviour and actions, his self frees itself from this trait and becomes content with obedience to Allāh (تَبَارَكَ وَتَعَالَىٰ) and his remembrance. It does not order its owner except to do virtuous acts, and its return will be to Allāh's (تَبَارَكَ وَتَعَالَىٰ) grace and reward. Allāh (تَبَارَكَ وَتَعَالَىٰ) said,

﴿ يَٰٓأَيَّتُهَا ٱلنَّفْسُ ٱلْمُطْمَئِنَّةُ ﴿٢٧﴾ ٱرْجِعِىٓ إِلَىٰ رَبِّكِ رَاضِيَةً مَّرْضِيَّةً ﴿٢٨﴾ فَٱدْخُلِى فِى عِبَٰدِى ﴿٢٩﴾ وَٱدْخُلِى جَنَّتِى ﴿٣٠﴾ ﴾

> **"You, content and fulfilled spirit! Return to your Lord delighted and delightful. Then enter amongst my slaves, and enter my paradise."**
>
> [*Sūrah Fajr* 89:27-39]

It is the individual's responsibility to strive for the rectification of his self and its deliverance from having this blameworthy nature – that it is an avid inciter to acts of evil. This is done through hard work and adopting the best behavioural traits, as well as constant prayer to Allāh (تَبَارَكَ وَتَعَالَىٰ) and frequent repetition of the following transmitted prayer:

> "Allāh! Guide me to the best character traits and actions, no one guides to the best of them except You, and save me from the worst character traits and actions. No one can save me from the worst of them except You."[15]

[15] Part of a *ḥadīth* collected by Muslim and narrated by Alī ibn Abī Ṭālib. See *ḥadīth* (no.771).

The Virtue of Knowledge

The details of this story show the advantage of being knowledgeable and illustrate the fact that through having it, one gains prestige in this life and the hereafter, as well as spiritual and material well-being. Yūsuf (عَلَيْهِ ٱلسَّلَامُ), for instance, did not obtain all that he did except due to the knowledge he possessed, which is why his farther said,

﴿ وَكَذَٰلِكَ يَجْتَبِيكَ رَبُّكَ وَيُعَلِّمُكَ مِن تَأْوِيلِ ٱلْأَحَادِيثِ ۝٦ ﴾

"And like that, your Lord shall choose you and teach you the interpretation of dreams."

[*Sūrah Yūsuf* 12:6]

Allāh (تَبَارَكَ وَتَعَالَىٰ) blessed him with free time to devote to the acquisition of knowledge while he was staying with the Azīz. With this knowledge, he attained the rank of excellence.

He also came out of prison with honour and respect due to his knowledge.

He gained authority with the king and he made him his personal favourite after he spoke to him and realised the extent of his knowledge.

He also used his knowledge to manage the affairs of the people in the kingdom of Egypt by rectifying their worldly affairs, and skilfully supervising the preservation, expenditure and distribution of the land's treasuries and stores.

Then at the end of his purpose, he appealed to his Lord by showing his appreciation for the knowledge He had given him, asking that He take care of his affairs in this life. In which instance He said,

﴿ رَبِّ قَدْ ءَاتَيْتَنِي مِنَ ٱلْمُلْكِ وَعَلَّمْتَنِي مِن تَأْوِيلِ ٱلْأَحَادِيثِ ۚ فَاطِرَ ٱلسَّمَٰوَٰتِ وَٱلْأَرْضِ أَنتَ
وَلِيِّۦ فِي ٱلدُّنْيَا وَٱلْآخِرَةِ ۖ تَوَفَّنِي مُسْلِمًا وَأَلْحِقْنِي بِٱلصَّٰلِحِينَ ﴿١٠١﴾ ﴾

"My Lord! You have indeed bestowed on me of the sovereignty, and taught me the interpretation of dreams; The (only) Creator of the heavens and the earth! You are my Wali (Protector, Helper, Supporter, Guardian, etc.) in this world and in the Hereafter, cause me to die as a Muslim (the one submitting to Your Will), and join me with the righteous."

[*Sūrah Yūsuf* 12:101]

Hence, the wonderful virtues and rewards of knowledge, whether immediate (in this life) or eventual (in the hereafter), are innumerable.

Divine Medicine

In this story is also evidence that the cure for diseases can be through divine causes, just as it can be through physical medicine. In fact, this type of cure produces the kind of results other types cannot.

Take, for instance, Ya'qūb (عَلَيْهِ ٱلسَّلَامُ). Grief had made his eyes fade and his eyesight had dwindled. Allāh (تَبَارَكَ وَتَعَالَىٰ) made Yūsuf's (عَلَيْهِ ٱلسَّلَامُ) shirt his cure and used it to return his eyesight when he laid it across his face. His eyesight flooded back because the scent of Yūsuf (عَلَيْهِ ٱلسَّلَامُ) was on it – the one over whom was the grief that caused the ailment in his eyes. It was such that his only cure, along with the kindness of Allāh (تَبَارَكَ وَتَعَالَىٰ), was in the shirt Yūsuf used to cover his body; and whoever says the shirt was, in fact, from Paradise, does not have an ounce of proof to support his claim. Allāh (تَبَارَكَ وَتَعَالَىٰ) is able to have cured him even without any medium or instrument, but He is Wise and so has made the flow of events dependant on causes and procedures that people sometimes understand and sometimes do not.

The Permissibility of Asking People, Especially Kings when Necessary

This story also shows the permissibility of begging people, especially kings, when necessary. This is due to what Yūsuf's brothers said:

﴿يَٰٓأَيُّهَا ٱلْعَزِيزُ مَسَّنَا وَأَهْلَنَا ٱلضُّرُّ وَجِئْنَا بِبِضَٰعَةٍ مُّزْجَىٰةٍ فَأَوْفِ لَنَا ٱلْكَيْلَ وَتَصَدَّقْ
عَلَيْنَآ ۖ إِنَّ ٱللَّهَ يَجْزِى ٱلْمُتَصَدِّقِينَ ﴿٨٨﴾﴾

"Dear Azīz! A hard time has hit us and our family, and we have brought but poor capital, so pay us full measure and be charitable to us. Truly, Allāh does reward the charitable."

[*Sūrah Yūsuf* 12:88]

Because they asked him for equity in his dealings with them and charity for which they would give nothing in exchange.

Furthermore, I only said, "especially kings", because kings are not asked to give from their own personal wealth but rather they are asked to give from the treasury, which is for public advantage, and the most important advantage is satisfying the needs of the desperate.

The Meaning of Ignorance

Another noteworthy point from this story is that "ignorance," just as it is may mean lack of knowledge, may also mean lack of restraint, as well as the act of sinning.

The proof is in His (تَبَارَكَ وَتَعَالَىٰ) statement:

﴿ قَالَ رَبِّ ٱلسِّجْنُ أَحَبُّ إِلَيَّ مِمَّا يَدْعُونَنِيٓ إِلَيْهِۖ وَإِلَّا تَصْرِفْ عَنِّي كَيْدَهُنَّ أَصْبُ إِلَيْهِنَّ وَأَكُن مِّنَ ٱلْجَٰهِلِينَ ﴿٣٣﴾ ﴾

"He said: "O' my Lord! Prison is more to my liking than that to which they invite me. Unless You turn away their plot from me, I will feel inclined towards them and be one (of those who commit sin and deserve blame or those who do deeds) of the ignorant."

[*Sūrah Yūsuf* 12:33]

And His (تَبَارَكَ وَتَعَالَىٰ) statement:

﴿ هَلْ عَلِمْتُم مَّا فَعَلْتُم بِيُوسُفَ وَأَخِيهِ إِذْ أَنتُمْ جَٰهِلُونَ ﴿٨٩﴾ ﴾

"Do you know what you did with Yūsuf (Joseph) and his brother, when you were ignorant?"

[*Sūrah Yūsuf* 12:89]

The meaning here is not "*a lack of knowledge*" but "*a lack of its application*" and "*being immersed in sin.*" The statement of Musā (عَلَيْهِ السَّلَامُ) is similar to it:

﴿ قَالَ أَعُوذُ بِٱللَّهِ أَنْ أَكُونَ مِنَ ٱلْجَٰهِلِينَ ﴾

"I seek refuge with Allāh lest I should be one of the ignorant."

[*Sūrah al-Baqarah* 2:67]

And Allāh's (تَبَارَكَ وَتَعَالَى) statement:

﴿ إِنَّمَا ٱلتَّوْبَةُ عَلَى ٱللَّهِ لِلَّذِينَ يَعْمَلُونَ ٱلسُّوٓءَ بِجَهَٰلَةٍ ثُمَّ يَتُوبُونَ مِن قَرِيبٍ ﴾

"It is only right for Allāh to accept the repentance of those who do evil in ignorance and repent early [before it is too late]."

[*Sūrah an-Nisā* 5:17]

Everyone who disobeys Allāh (تَبَارَكَ وَتَعَالَى) is ignorant from the aspect of not implementing knowledge, because true knowledge is the kind by which ignorance vanishes and the kind that compels to action.

"Whoever Brings it Gets [the Reward of] a Camel Load, and on that You have My Word."

Another point of note is Allāh's (تَبَارَكَ وَتَعَالَى) statement,

﴿ وَلِمَن جَآءَ بِهِۦ حِمۡلُ بَعِيرٖ وَأَنَا۠ بِهِۦ زَعِيمٞ ﴾

"And for him who produces it is (the reward of) a camel load; I will be bound by it [my word]."

[*Sūrah Yūsuf* 12:72]

This verse was used as evidence for three branches of Jurisprudence:

- the topic of wages,
- the topic of guarantee,
- and the topic of surety.

This is because His (تَبَارَكَ وَتَعَالَى) statement,

﴿ وَلِمَن جَآءَ بِهِۦ حِمۡلُ بَعِيرٖ وَأَنَا۠ بِهِۦ زَعِيمٞ ﴾

"And for him who produces it is (the reward of) a camel load; I will be bound by it [my word]."

[*Sūrah Yūsuf* 12:72]

is an expression of some type of wage. A wage is as an offer to someone of something familiar, such as a camel load, or the like, as custom demands, in exchange for a defined or undefined task. It is permissible due to the advantages that it offers both the employer and the worker.

Additionally, His (سُبْحَانَهُ وَتَعَالَىٰ) statement:

﴿ وَأَنَا۠ بِهِۦ زَعِيمٌ ﴾

"I will be bound by it."

[*Sūrah Yūsuf* 12:72]

That is, I guarantee this payment and I am liable for it, and it is one of the transactions that secure the rights by which the expansion of dealings and their rectification becomes fulfilled.

Reformation is Achieved by the Implementation of Islamic Law

Another significant point obtained from this story is that in the implementation of Islamic law lies the reform of the land and country, as well as its stability. While its detriment lies in actions of disobedience, such as theft and so on. The proof for this is that they said:

﴿تَٱللَّهِ لَقَدْ عَلِمْتُم مَّا جِئْنَا لِنُفْسِدَ فِى ٱلْأَرْضِ وَمَا كُنَّا سَٰرِقِينَ ﴿٧٣﴾﴾

"By Allāh! Indeed you know that we came not to make mischief in the land, and we are no thieves!"
[*Sūrah Yūsuf* 12:73]

Added to that, how many instances are there in the Qur'ān of the explicit statement that actions of disobedience and defiance towards the messengers are a detriment to the land, and that general welfare lies in following the messengers – both in religious and material affairs.

For Every Soul is what it has Earned

The story also contains proof of the fundamental principle that Allāh (تَبَارَكَ وَتَعَالَى) expressed and echoed in His Book: that for every soul is all that it earned of good and reward, and against it is all that it brought upon itself of evil and punishment, and that no soul shall carry the burden of another.

From His (سُبْحَانَهُ وَتَعَالَى) statement,

﴿قَالَ مَعَاذَ ٱللَّهِ أَن نَّأْخُذَ إِلَّا مَن وَجَدْنَا مَتَٰعَنَا عِندَهُۥٓ إِنَّآ إِذًا لَّظَٰلِمُونَ ﴿٧٩﴾﴾

"He said: "Allāh forbid, that we should take anyone but him with whom we found our property. Indeed (if we did so), we should be wrong-doers."

[*Sūrah Yūsuf* 12:79]

Perform Actions that Lead to Good and Protect You Against Adversities

The story contains many examples that prove this fundamental principle, and the ideal approach is to take necessary measures while seeking Allāh's (تَبَارَكَ وَتَعَالَى) help and trusting Him. Ya'qūb (عَلَيْهِ ٱلسَّلَامُ) took every possible precaution in protecting his children – first for Yūsuf (عَلَيْهِ ٱلسَّلَامُ), then for his brother when he sent him with his older brothers - and he further said,

﴿ فَٱللَّهُ خَيْرٌ حَـٰفِظًا ۖ وَهُوَ أَرْحَمُ ٱلرَّٰحِمِينَ ﴾

"But Allāh is the Best to guard, and He is the Most Merciful of those who show mercy."

[*Sūrah Yūsuf* 12:64]

It is incumbent upon the individual, when he is burdened with problems and invaded by misfortunes, to exercise patience and seek Allāh's (تَبَارَكَ وَتَعَالَى) help in overcoming them. Ya'qūb (عَلَيْهِ ٱلسَّلَامُ) said, after

Yūsuf's brothers did what they did to him and the greatest of calamities overtook him,

﴿ وَٱللَّهُ ٱلْمُسْتَعَانُ عَلَىٰ مَا تَصِفُونَ ﴾

"And it is Allāh (Alone) Whose help can be sought against that which you assert."

[*Sūrah Yūsuf* 12:18]

That is because one cannot totally endure in keeping to obedient acts, staying away from forbidden acts and standing firm in the face of calamities or be saved, except by seeking Allāh's (تَبَارَكَ وَتَعَالَىٰ) help, and an individual should never depend on himself. Yūsuf (عَلَيْهِ ٱلسَّلَامُ) said,

﴿ قَالَ رَبِّ ٱلسِّجْنُ أَحَبُّ إِلَيَّ مِمَّا يَدْعُونَنِيٓ إِلَيْهِ ۖ وَإِلَّا تَصْرِفْ عَنِّي كَيْدَهُنَّ أَصْبُ إِلَيْهِنَّ
وَأَكُن مِّنَ ٱلْجَٰهِلِينَ ﴿٣٣﴾ ﴾

"Unless You turn away their plot from me, I will feel inclined towards them and be one (of those who commit sin and deserve blame or those who do deeds) of the ignorant."

[*Sūrah Yūsuf* 12:33]

Methods of Debate

This story also teaches the advantageous debate method of making comparisons between the truth and falsehood.

It works by demonstrating the virtues of the truth and its immediate and future benefits, as opposed to the nature of falsehood, which is a combination of all the things that are contrary to that.

Allāh (تَبَارَكَ وَتَعَالَىٰ) says, while referring to Yūsuf's (عَلَيْهِ ٱلسَّلَامُ) call to the belief in the singularity of Allāh (تَبَارَكَ وَتَعَالَىٰ):

﴿ يَٰصَٰحِبَيِ ٱلسِّجْنِ ءَأَرْبَابٌ مُّتَفَرِّقُونَ خَيْرٌ أَمِ ٱللَّهُ ٱلْوَٰحِدُ ٱلْقَهَّارُ ٣٩ ﴾

"My fellow inmates! Are many different lords (gods) better or Allāh, the One, the Irresistible?"

[*Sūrah Yūsuf* 12:39]

Then he mentioned the nature of *shirk* (worshipping others besides or along with Allāh) and its vileness and wretchedness, and how it is based on following false conjectures. That every group that practises *shirk* has its own particular object of worship – whether it be fire, a statue, a grave, the dead or any other thing from amongst their objects of worship that can neither help nor harm themselves or their worshippers any way, and can neither cause death nor give life nor resurrect the dead. Moreover, each group believes the others to be wrong, while in fact they are all wrong and headed towards destruction. Are these [false] lords and objects of worship better, or Allāh, the One, the Absolute Commander [of everything]?

Then he mentioned three great, universal attributes belonging to Allāh (تَبَارَكَ وَتَعَالَى):

1. He is Allāh (تَبَارَكَ وَتَعَالَى), the One who alone bears and deserves the most exalted names and attributes. All blessings are from Him, and for that reason does Allāh (تَبَارَكَ وَتَعَالَى) deserve to be the only entity of worship, the God of the occupants of heaven and earth, and He is the One who is God in Heaven and God on earth.

2. He is the One, the only one who possesses all the attributes of perfection, the one who singularly possesses the attributes of majesty and beauty, and who has no one who collaborates with Him in any of the things that He does.

3. He is the Absolute Commander of everything. This means that all of the heavenly and netherworlds are dominated by His power, subject to His majesty, humbled by His might and omnipotence (تَبَارَكَ وَتَعَالَى). Therefore, the one who possesses these amazing attributes is the one alone, without any partner, besides whom it is inappropriate to worship anything.

The Proper Religion

The story points out that the proper religion, the one practised by all the messengers [of Allāh] and their followers, is the worship of Allāh alone (تَبَارَكَ وَتَعَالَىٰ), to the exclusion of anything else besides Him. This is evident in His words,

﴿لِلَّهِ أَمَرَ أَلَّا تَعْبُدُوٓا۟ إِلَّآ إِيَّاهُ ۚ ذَٰلِكَ ٱلدِّينُ ٱلْقَيِّمُ وَلَٰكِنَّ أَكْثَرَ ٱلنَّاسِ لَا يَعْلَمُونَ﴾

“The command (or the judgement) is for none but Allāh. He has commanded that you worship none but Him (i.e. His Monotheism), that is the (true) straight religion, but most men know not”

[*Sūrah Yūsuf* 12:40]

It is the proper religion, which rectifies character, beliefs and actions. It is the one without which there can be no integrity in either material or spiritual affairs.

The Obligation of Acknowledging Allāh's Blessings

This story also shows the obligation of acknowledging Allāh's (تَبَارَكَ وَتَعَالَىٰ) spiritual and material blessings.

He says,

﴿ ذَٰلِكَ مِن فَضْلِ ٱللَّهِ عَلَيْنَا ﴾

"This is from the Grace of Allāh to us."

[*Sūrah Yūsuf* 12:38]

This is because He is the One who bestowed the blessings of well-being and provision, as well as the things that depend on them. He is the One who bestowed the blessings of Islām, faith and obedience to him, as well as the things that depend on them. An individual should therefore acknowledge these blessings inside his heart, tell others about them, and use to them to help him in obeying his benefactor.

Ways of Obtaining Knowledge and Blessings

Yūsuf's (عَلَيْهِ السَّلَامُ) story also shows that excelling in the worship of Allāh (تَبَارَكَ وَتَعَالَىٰ) and being good to His slaves is a way through which one may obtain knowledge and obtain the blessings of this life and the next. This is evident in His statement,

﴿ وَلَقَدْ هَمَّتْ بِهِۦ ۖ وَهَمَّ بِهَا لَوْلَآ أَن رَّءَا بُرْهَـٰنَ رَبِّهِۦ ۚ كَذَٰلِكَ لِنَصْرِفَ عَنْهُ ٱلسُّوٓءَ وَٱلْفَحْشَآءَ ۚ إِنَّهُۥ مِنْ عِبَادِنَا ٱلْمُخْلَصِينَ ٢٤ ﴾

"And when he [Yūsuf (Joseph)] attained his full manhood, We gave him wisdom and knowledge (the Prophethood), thus We reward the Muḥsinūn."

[*Sūrah Yūsuf* 12:22]

Further, His (تَبَارَكَ وَتَعَالَىٰ) statement,

﴿ وَكَذَٰلِكَ مَكَّنَّا لِيُوسُفَ فِى ٱلْأَرْضِ يَتَبَوَّأُ مِنْهَا حَيْثُ يَشَآءُ نُصِيبُ بِرَحْمَتِنَا مَن نَّشَآءُ وَلَا نُضِيعُ أَجْرَ ٱلْمُحْسِنِينَ ﴿٥٦﴾ وَلَأَجْرُ ٱلْءَاخِرَةِ خَيْرٌ لِّلَّذِينَ ءَامَنُوا۟ وَكَانُوا۟ يَتَّقُونَ ﴿٥٧﴾ ﴾

"Thus did We give full authority to Yūsuf (Joseph) in the land, to take possession therein, as when or where he likes. We bestow of Our Mercy on whom We please, and We make not to be lost the reward of Al-Muḥsinūn. And verily, the reward of the Hereafter is better for those who believe and used to fear Allāh and keep their duty to Him (by abstaining from all kinds of sins and evil deeds and by performing all kinds of righteous good deeds)."

[*Sūrah Yūsuf* 12:56-57]

Thus, Allāh (تَبَارَكَ وَتَعَالَىٰ) made excellence in the practice of good deeds the reason for the achievement of these elevated ranks.

Looking Forward to One's Desired Goals

Looking forward to one's desired goals makes it easy to bear any difficulties that may appear on the path to achieving them. Whenever an individual knows the outcome to an event, and that it eventually ends well for him in this life and the next, its difficulties become easy for him to bear, and he finds consolation in his knowledge of the eventual conclusion – as indicated by His statement – the Exalted One:

﴿ فَلَمَّا ذَهَبُوا۟ بِهِۦ وَأَجْمَعُوٓا۟ أَن يَجْعَلُوهُ فِى غَيَٰبَتِ ٱلْجُبِّ ۚ وَأَوْحَيْنَآ إِلَيْهِ لَتُنَبِّئَنَّهُم بِأَمْرِهِمْ
هَٰذَا وَهُمْ لَا يَشْعُرُونَ ﴿١٥﴾ ﴾

"So, when they took him away, they all agreed to throw him down to the bottom of the well, and We inspired in him:" Indeed, you shall (one day) inform them of this their affair, when they know (you) not."

[*Sūrah Yūsuf* 12:15]

It was revealed to Yūsuf, under those stressful circumstances that these current events will lead you to a good and comfortable life; and that after this humiliation by your brothers, you will eventually be favoured above them and come to a praiseworthy end. This revelation has a combination of some of the greatest of Allāh's (تَبَارَكَ وَتَعَالَىٰ) blessings to any worshipper: kindness, consolation and help in easing affliction.

It is for this great purpose that Allāh (تَبَارَكَ وَتَعَالَىٰ) reminds His slaves during difficult and stressful situations that they lead to the obtainment of His reward and His blessings, and instil yearning for His favour. Allāh (تَبَارَكَ وَتَعَالَىٰ) says:

﴿إِن تَكُونُوا۟ تَأْلَمُونَ فَإِنَّهُمْ يَأْلَمُونَ كَمَا تَأْلَمُونَ ۖ وَتَرْجُونَ مِنَ ٱللَّهِ مَا لَا يَرْجُونَ ۗ﴾

"If you hurt, then [know that] they hurt just like you hurt, yet you hope from Allāh what they do not hope for."

[*Sūrah an-Nisa* 6:104]

His (تَبَارَكَ وَتَعَالَىٰ) statement:

﴿وَأَجْمَعُوٓا۟ أَن يَجْعَلُوهُ فِى غَيَٰبَتِ ٱلْجُبِّ ۚ﴾

"They all agreed to throw him down to the bottom of the well."

[*Sūrah Yūsuf* 12:15]

Is evidence that they all reverted to the opinion of the one who said:

﴿لَا تَقْتُلُوا۟ يُوسُفَ وَأَلْقُوهُ فِى غَيَٰبَتِ ٱلْجُبِّ﴾

"Kill not Yūsuf (Joseph), but if you must do something, throw him down to the bottom of a well."

[*Sūrah Yūsuf* 12:10]

The same way His (تَبَارَكَ وَتَعَالَىٰ) statement:

﴿ وَإِلَّا تَصْرِفْ عَنِّي كَيْدَهُنَّ أَصْبُ إِلَيْهِنَّ وَأَكُن مِّنَ الْجَاهِلِينَ ﴿٣٣﴾ فَاسْتَجَابَ لَهُ رَبُّهُ ﴿٣٤﴾ ﴾

"Unless You turn away their plot from me, I will feel inclined towards them and be one (of those who commit sin and deserve blame or those who do deeds) of the ignorant. So his Lord answered his invocation and turned away from him their plot."

[*Sūrah Yūsuf* 12:33-34]

Is evidence that the women helped al-Azīz's wife against Yūsuf, and began to tempt him to commit the act she wanted from him. After they saw what they saw of Yūsuf's (عَلَيْهِ السَّلَامُ) immense beauty, they became al-Azīz's wife's accomplices, even though earlier they had reprimanded her saying,

﴿ وَقَالَ نِسْوَةٌ فِي الْمَدِينَةِ امْرَأَتُ الْعَزِيزِ تُرَاوِدُ فَتَاهَا عَن نَّفْسِهِ ۖ قَدْ شَغَفَهَا حُبًّا ۖ إِنَّا لَنَرَاهَا
فِي ضَلَالٍ مُّبِينٍ ﴿٣٠﴾ ﴾

"And women in the city said: "The wife of Al-'Azīz is seeking to seduce her (slave) young man, indeed she loves him violently; verily we see her in plain error!"

[*Sūrah Yūsuf* 12:30]

Actions or Statements Can Imply Agreements

The story proves that actions or statements can form agreements implied by them, there being no difference between charity agreements and trade agreements.

The evidence for this is that Yūsuf (عَلَيْهِ ٱلسَّلَامُ) gave his brothers back the possession of the merchandise that they used to buy their rations without them noticing. When they opened their goods, they found their merchandise in their luggage and they were happy with that – as mentioned in the verse. This all took place without any verbal consent or acceptance. This is because the act and the approval of the act point to an agreement.

How Could Yūsuf's Whereabouts be Unknown to Ya'qūb?

If one were to ask the question:

How could Yūsuf's (عَلَيْهِ ٱلسَّلَامُ) whereabouts be unknown to Ya'qūb (عَلَيْهِ ٱلسَّلَامُ) for such a long period of time when there was nothing but a short distance between them, and despite the strong and persistent urge to find him, his knowledge that he was alive and his fervent desire to meet him?

The answer is:

It is not surprising that Allāh (تَبَارَكَ وَتَعَالَى) can do this. This is because even if there are indeed very strong forces at work, they are in no way outside Allāh's decree and power. Allāh (تَبَارَكَ وَتَعَالَى) wanted that the reunion should not be until the time to which He postponed it, and under the circumstances that He wanted, due to some great wisdom. Whenever Allāh (تَبَارَكَ وَتَعَالَى) wants something to be at a specific time, He assigns material or immaterial forces that prevent it from happening before its set time, the same way He assigns the forces that bring about what He wants. All forces are in the Hands of Allāh (تَبَارَكَ وَتَعَالَىٰ). This incident is not stranger than the case of the children of Isrā'īl (i.e. the Jews) when they were in the wilderness, and they were a huge nation of people, while the wilderness covered only a small area of land and they were between many villages and cities. For a forty-year period, they could not find a way to their destination and they could not find anyone to guide them to their purpose.

Similar to that are the people of the cave. They stayed for three hundred and nine years in a cave close to a huge city, yet for a purpose that Allāh (تَبَارَكَ وَتَعَالَىٰ) wanted to fulfil, no one came across them in this extended stretch of time. These events and others like them are evidence of Allāh's (تَبَارَكَ وَتَعَالَىٰ) absolute power and wisdom. Only Allāh knows how long Yūsuf stayed in al-Azīz's house, then in prison, then he was promoted to managing the kingdom. Who would have thought that he would go from slavery and imprisonment to such great authority?

Furthermore, it is most likely that at the time he gained authority, he become known to the people by his title as the king's viceroy, and almost no one knew his name, which is mostly the case with kings and such people. This is why his brothers came to him time after time and he knew them while they did not know him because he was in all the splendour of his authority. Additionally, they parted from him while he was young and did not see him until after he had grown old. It is well known that a person's features change when he reaches middle age. Allāh (تَبَارَكَ وَتَعَالَىٰ) knows best.

That is from the perspective of Ya'qūb (عَلَيْهِ السَّلَامُ) and his sons. As for Yūsuf (عَلَيْهِ السَّلَامُ), he already knew where his family was and intentionally delayed meeting them until the appropriate time, which is why although his brothers came to him time after time and he had recognised them, he did not let them know who he was and he did not invite his parents and family until the end.

How to Face Adversities

We draw from Allāh's (تَبَارَكَ وَتَعَالَىٰ) statement, quoting Ya'qūb (عَلَيْهِ السَّلَامُ) regarding what Yūsuf's brothers first did to him,

﴿ قَالَ بَلْ سَوَّلَتْ لَكُمْ أَنفُسُكُمْ أَمْرًا ﴾

"He [Ya'qūb (Jacob)] said: "Rather, your ownselves have beguiled you into something."

[*Sūrah Yūsuf* 12:83]

And his statement when the matter became serious - when his other son was detained:

﴿ فَصَبْرٌ جَمِيلٌ عَسَى ٱللَّهُ أَن يَأْتِيَنِي بِهِمْ جَمِيعًا إِنَّهُۥ هُوَ ٱلْعَلِيمُ ٱلْحَكِيمُ ﴾

"So patience is most fitting (for me). Maybe Allāh will bring them (back) all to me. Truly He! only He is All-Knowing, All-Wise.."

[*Sūrah Yūsuf* 12:83]

These verses point to the fact that when troubles and adversities hit Allāh's chosen ones, they face them in the first instance by exercising patience and seeking the help of the Protector. Later on, at the end, when the strain of the adversity has reached its maximum, they face it with endurance and the hope of relief. Thus, Allāh (تَبَارَكَ وَتَعَالَىٰ) makes it possible for them to fulfil the obligations of their devotion to Him in both instances.

Then, once Allāh (تَبَارَكَ وَتَعَالَىٰ) has taken away their adversity, they receive His aid with gratitude and praise for Him and a deeper understanding of His kindness, as indicated by Yūsuf's (عَلَيْهِ السَّلَامُ) words,

﴿وَقَالَ يَٰٓأَبَتِ هَٰذَا تَأْوِيلُ رُءْيَٰىَ مِن قَبْلُ قَدْ جَعَلَهَا رَبِّى حَقًّا ۖ وَقَدْ أَحْسَنَ بِىٓ إِذْ أَخْرَجَنِى
مِنَ ٱلسِّجْنِ وَجَآءَ بِكُم مِّنَ ٱلْبَدْوِ مِنۢ بَعْدِ أَن نَّزَغَ ٱلشَّيْطَٰنُ بَيْنِى وَبَيْنَ إِخْوَتِىٓ ۚ إِنَّ رَبِّى
لَطِيفٌ لِّمَا يَشَآءُ ۚ إِنَّهُۥ هُوَ ٱلْعَلِيمُ ٱلْحَكِيمُ ۝١٠٠﴾

"He said: Dear father, this is the interpretation of my dream aforetime! My Lord has made it come true! He was indeed good to me, when He took me out of the prison, and brought you (all here) out of the Bedouin-life, after Shaitān (Satan) had sown enmity between me and my brothers. Certainly, my Lord is the Most Courteous and Kind unto whom He will. Truly He! Only He is the All-Knowing, the All-Wise."

[*Sūrah Yūsuf* 12:100]

No Burdened Soul Should Carry the Sins of Another

Allāh (تَبَارَكَ وَتَعَالَى) says,

﴿قَالَ مَعَاذَ ٱللَّهِ أَن نَّأْخُذَ إِلَّا مَن وَجَدْنَا مَتَٰعَنَا عِندَهُۥٓ إِنَّآ إِذًا لَّظَٰلِمُونَ ۝٧٩﴾

"He said: "Allāh forbid, that we should take anyone but him with whom we found our property. Indeed (if we did so), we should be wrong-doers."

[*Sūrah Yūsuf* 12:79]

The verse shows that no soul should carry the sins of another. Moreover, a very subtle principle can be deduced from this: kindness is only kindness when it does not involve doing a forbidden act or neglecting to do an obligatory one. Yūsuf's brothers asked Yūsuf (عَلَيْهِ ٱلسَّلَامُ) to be kind to them by allowing his brother to return to his father and to take one of them instead of him, but he refused and said:

﴿ قَالَ مَعَاذَ ٱللَّهِ أَن نَّأْخُذَ إِلَّا مَن وَجَدْنَا مَتَٰعَنَا عِندَهُۥٓ إِنَّآ إِذًا لَّظَٰلِمُونَ ﴿٧٩﴾ ﴾

"He said: "Allāh forbid, that we should take anyone but him with whom we found our property. Indeed (if we did so), we should be wrong-doers."

[*Sūrah Yūsuf* 12:79]

Hence, if a kindness involves abandoning justice, it becomes oppression. This is why showing favouritism towards some children above others and to some wives above others is forbidden even though it might be kindness towards the one being preferred and favoured, because it is an act of injustice. Any such act follows the same rule. Allāh (تَبَارَكَ وَتَعَالَىٰ) knows best.

Seeking the Truth

The story also teaches that the only ones who benefit from Allāh's (تَبَارَكَ وَتَعَالَىٰ) signs, whichever they may be, are the guided seekers whose aims are to learn and follow the truth. This is indicated by His statement,

﴿ لَّقَدْ كَانَ فِي يُوسُفَ وَإِخْوَتِهِۦٓ ءَايَٰتٌ لِّلسَّآئِلِينَ ﴾

"Verily, in Yūsuf (Joseph) and his brethren, there were *Ayāt* (proofs, evidences, verses, lessons, signs, revelations, etc.) for those who ask."

[*Sūrah Yūsuf* 12:7]

As for the heedless people who turn away, or the opposing, obstinate ones, then the following statement of Allāh (تَبَارَكَ وَتَعَالَىٰ) applies to them:

﴿ فَلَمَّآ أَن جَآءَ ٱلْبَشِيرُ أَلْقَىٰهُ عَلَىٰ وَجْهِهِۦ فَٱرْتَدَّ بَصِيرًا ۖ قَالَ أَلَمْ أَقُل لَّكُمْ إِنِّىٓ أَعْلَمُ
مِنَ ٱللَّهِ مَا لَا تَعْلَمُونَ ﴿٩٦﴾ قَالُوا۟ يَٰٓأَبَانَا ٱسْتَغْفِرْ لَنَا ذُنُوبَنَآ إِنَّا كُنَّا خَٰطِـِٔينَ ﴿٩٧﴾ ﴾

"Then, when the bearer of the glad tidings arrived, he cast it (the shirt) over his face, and he became clear-sighted. He said: "Did I not say to you, 'I know from Allāh that which you know not. They said: "O' our father! Ask forgiveness (from Allāh) for our sins, indeed we have been sinners."

[*Sūrah Yūsuf* 12:96-97]

So contemplating Allāh's (تَبَارَكَ وَتَعَالَىٰ) spoken verses and natural signs benefits anyone whose aim is the truth.

Allāh (تَبَارَكَ وَتَعَالَىٰ) also said:

﴿ يَهْدِي بِهِ اللَّهُ مَنِ اتَّبَعَ رِضْوَانَهُ سُبُلَ السَّلَامِ ﴾

"Allāh guides with it whoever follows that which pleases him to the paths of peace."

[*Sūrah al-Mā'idah* 6:16]

There are so many places in the Qur'ān where Allāh (تَبَارَكَ وَتَعَالَىٰ) attaches the possibility of benefitting from His verses to this condition.

For example:

﴿ إِنَّ فِي ذَٰلِكَ لَآيَةً لِّلْمُؤْمِنِينَ ﴿٧٧﴾ ﴾

"Indeed, in that are signs for the believers,"

[*Sūrah Ḥijr* 15:77]

And;

﴿ وَفِي ٱلۡأَرۡضِ ءَايَٰتٞ لِّلۡمُوقِنِينَ ﴿٢٠﴾ ﴾

"Indeed, on the earth are signs for those with certainty,"

[*Sūrah adh-Dhāriyāt* 12:20]

And;

﴿ لَقَدۡ كَانَ فِي قَصَصِهِمۡ عِبۡرَةٞ لِّأُوْلِي ٱلۡأَلۡبَٰبِۗ ﴾

"Truly, there is a lesson in their stories for people who understand."

[*Sūrah Yūsuf* 12:111]

And;

﴿ يُقَلِّبُ ٱللَّهُ ٱلَّيۡلَ وَٱلنَّهَارَۚ إِنَّ فِي ذَٰلِكَ لَعِبۡرَةٗ لِّأُوْلِي ٱلۡأَبۡصَٰرِ ﴾

"Allāh alternates the day and night. Indeed, in that are signs for people with insight."

[*Sūrah Nūr* 51:44]

Seeking Counsel is Always Beneficial

This story also shows that seeking counsel is always advantageous, even when the aim is to mitigate an evil. This is why Yūsuf's brothers consulted with one another regarding what to do with him - should it be murder or should they dump him in some far away land? After which they agreed on the suggestion of the one who directed them to throw him into the depths of the well, in hope that some caravan would pick him up. In this incident, there is support for the well-known principle: doing the lesser of two evils is better than doing the greater one.

Likewise, when the detainment of the one in whose luggage the cup was found became a fixed decision, and they tried to persuade Yūsuf (عَلَيْهِ ٱلسَّلَامُ) to take a substitute for him - because they knew how hard it would be on their father – but he refused, they withdrew, and huddled together in private discourse and mutual consultation. They thereafter settled on the opinion of the eldest one of them: that he should remain in Egypt and keep up with his brother's situation. Meanwhile, they would go and provide for their family and inform their father about the details of the case. There is no doubt too that his remaining in Egypt was easier on Ya'qūb (عَلَيْهِ ٱلسَّلَامُ) and increased his hope of achieving his desire. His act was also sort of like him sharing in the ordeal of his two brothers, Yūsuf (عَلَيْهِ السَّلَامُ) and Benyāmīn, and this is why Ya'qūb (عَلَيْهِ السَّلَامُ) said,

﴿ عَسَى ٱللَّهُ أَن يَأْتِيَنِى بِهِمْ جَمِيعًا ﴾

"Maybe Allāh will bring them all back to me."

[*Sūrah Yūsuf* 12:83]

The Reason Ya'qūb Did Not Believe His Children

The only reason why Ya'qūb (عَلَيْهِ ٱلسَّلَامُ) did not believe his children when they said, '*a wolf ate him*', and fabricated the clues that would prove their innocence, was because doubt and false suggestions cannot contend with the truth. He had already known for a fact, through Yūsuf's (عَلَيْهِ ٱلسَّلَامُ) dream, and perhaps through other things, what Yūsuf's (عَلَيْهِ ٱلسَّلَامُ) outcome would be in terms of the blessings that would be fulfilled for him and the family of Ya'qūb (عَلَيْهِ ٱلسَّلَامُ). This also shows that one should not be deceived by simply the face value of the evidence.

There was a time when a woman and her disputant came to Shuraih and her eyes flooded with tears. One of the people present said;

> "I do not think except that the poor woman has been wronged."

Shuraih replied;

> "Have you not heard of the story of Yūsuf's brothers, when they came to their father in the evening crying?

> Were they wronged or were they the ones who did the wronging?"

How many people have been deluded and how many facts have been twisted due to these kind of falsifications? This is why the intelligent consider every scenario in an event and look at matters from every direction and every extreme.

Qualities of the Ruler

The story also shows that for all large and small governments, the person ruling them must be adequately strong, trustworthy and knowledgeable in the aspects of leadership.

Evidence of this is from the time when the king spoke to Yūsuf (عَلَيْهِ السَّلَامُ) and saw some of his knowledge, his experience of events, and his good insight, and he made him his personal favourite and said,

﴿ قَالَ إِنَّكَ ٱلْيَوْمَ لَدَيْنَا مَكِينٌ أَمِينٌ ﴾

> **"Verily, this day, you are with us high in rank and fully trusted."**
>
> [*Sūrah Yūsuf* 12:54]

Yūsuf (عَلَيْهِ السَّلَامُ) then said,

﴿ قَالَ ٱجْعَلْنِي عَلَىٰ خَزَآئِنِ ٱلْأَرْضِ إِنِّي حَفِيظٌ عَلِيمٌ ﴿٥٥﴾ ﴾

"Set me over the storehouses of the land; I will indeed guard them with full knowledge (as a minister of finance in Egypt, in place of al-'Azīz who was dead at that time)."

[*Sūrah Yūsuf* 12:55]

He gave his reason for deserving to be placed in charge to be his total efficiency in conserving whatever was under his responsibility and at his disposal, his full knowledge of the avenues of generating wealth and spending it, and the excellence of his management capabilities.

Furthermore, this is not an initial solicitation from Yūsuf for power, as many scholars state. Rather, when he saw that the king chose him and gave him authority over the affairs of the state, and that all the affairs were under his power and management, he asked the king to place him in charge over just the stores and treasuries. This is because they were more important, and because he knew that for him to take control of them would be more advantageous to the king and the people. This shows his total sincerity and the accuracy of his judgement.

The Qur'ān is Free of Falsehood or Mistakes

After Allāh (تَبَارَكَ وَتَعَالَىٰ) finished narrating this amazing story in detail, He said at the end of it,

﴿ لَقَدْ كَانَ فِي قَصَصِهِمْ عِبْرَةٌ لِّأُولِي الْأَلْبَابِ ۗ مَا كَانَ حَدِيثًا يُفْتَرَىٰ وَلَٰكِن
تَصْدِيقَ الَّذِي بَيْنَ يَدَيْهِ وَتَفْصِيلَ كُلِّ شَيْءٍ وَهُدًى وَرَحْمَةً لِّقَوْمٍ يُؤْمِنُونَ ﴿١١١﴾ ﴾

"Indeed in their stories, there is a lesson for men of understanding. It (the Qur'ān) is not a forged statement but a confirmation of Allāh's existing Books [the *Taurāt* (Torah), the *Injīl* (Gospel) and other Scriptures of Allāh] and a detailed explanation of everything and a guide and a Mercy for the people who believe."

[*Sūrah Yūsuf* 12:111]

Thus, He absolved the Qur'ān of having any sort of falsehood or mistake. Furthermore, He (تَبَارَكَ وَتَعَالَىٰ) described it using three attributes, in every one of them is the most compelling evidence that the Qur'ān is from Allāh (تَبَارَكَ وَتَعَالَىٰ), and that it is the truth without any doubt.

The first attribute is that it agrees with that which came before it, that is, with the books that were sent down from heaven and with the speech of the infallible messengers relaying what Allāh (تَبَارَكَ وَتَعَالَىٰ) revealed to them. As the Exalted One said,

﴿ بَلْ جَآءَ بِٱلْحَقِّ وَصَدَّقَ ٱلْمُرْسَلِينَ ﴿٣٧﴾ ﴾

"Actually, he came with the truth and attests to the truth of the messengers."

[*Sūrah Ṣafāt* 37:37]

Hence, this Qur'ān that Muḥammad (صَلَّى ٱللَّهُ عَلَيْهِ وَسَلَّمَ) brought came with the truth, and it is truthful in its information about Allāh (تَبَارَكَ وَتَعَالَىٰ), His angels, the Day of Judgment, and all past and future matters of the unknown. Its laws are just; it does not command except what is good, and it does not forbid except what is evil. As Allāh (تَبَارَكَ وَتَعَالَىٰ) said,

﴿ وَتَمَّتْ كَلِمَتُ رَبِّكَ صِدْقًا وَعَدْلًا ﴾

"And the word of your Lord is completely truth and just."

[*Sūrah al-An'ām* 6:115]

That is, it is completely true in its report and the justice of its laws, obligations and prohibitions.

There is no doubt that this Qur'ān, as well as confirming the truth of all the things that the messengers came with, also became a guardian over those things, and agreed with them in their fundamental principles and their important general comprehensive laws. In addition to that, the messengers in fact informed and brought good news of the coming of Muḥammad and what Muḥammad (ﷺ) brought. Thus, its informer spoke the truth and its prophecy came true.

The second attribute is that it is a detailed explanation of everything, and this includes everything that people need, in their beliefs, morals, and their external and internal actions, as well as in their religion and in their material affairs. For through it, Allāh (تَبَارَكَ وَتَعَالَى) has explained and given details of monotheism, the message and the recompense, as well as all the correct and true beliefs with an explanation and analysis that cannot be matched in its extensiveness by any book whatsoever. In it, He went into detail in His encouragement of performing the essential aspects of faith, and in the adoption of beautiful characteristics and the avoidance of lowly forms of character, and He explained the way and the means to attain the best of characteristics and repel the worst of them.

Similarly, He outlined the laws of the observable deeds, righteous actions, the permissible and the forbidden, and the good and the evil. He also outlined in it all advantageous aims and objectives, both religious and materialistic, and explained the means to achieving them.

In addition, He (تَبَارَكَ وَتَعَالَى) outlined in it by using logic as well as divine (revealed) proofs.

The third attribute is that it is guidance and a mercy for people who believe. Allāh (تَبَارَكَ وَتَعَالَى) uses it to guide those who follow that which pleases Him to the paths to salvation.

﴿ إِنَّ هَٰذَا ٱلْقُرْءَانَ يَهْدِى لِلَّتِى هِىَ أَقْوَمُ ﴾

"No doubt this Qur'ān guides to that which is the most upright."

[*Sūrah al-'Isrā* 17:9]

That is, it guides to every upright condition and straight path. It guides to the best actions and behaviour, and it guides to all advantageous aspects of the religion and all the beneficial aspects of the material world that are needed to observe the religion, and achieve complete happiness. The difference between guidance and mercy is that guidance involves the means and the ways that convey one to the good things of this life and the next one, while mercy is itself those good things, and is reward, both future and immediate. Hence, happiness in this life and the hereafter depends on following this Qur'ān in action and understanding.

Allāh (تَبَارَكَ وَتَعَالَى) specifically gave the believers' guidance and mercy because they are the ones who, in reality, profited from Allāh's (تَبَارَكَ وَتَعَالَى) guidance. They followed the guidance due to their faith and as a result, Allāh (تَبَارَكَ وَتَعَالَى) increased them in guidance and mercy.

Therefore, this Qur'ān is enlightenment for all people, showing them everything they need. There is, as a result, not an ounce of good anywhere except that it guides them to it and no evil except that it warns them against it. Through it, the proof has been established against all, yet it is guidance and a mercy for people who believe.

O' Allāh! Favor us with true faith, and make this Qur'ān for us a guidance and a mercy, indeed You are the Near One, the One who Responds to Prayer. May Allāh (تَبَارَكَ وَتَعَالَى) raise the repute of the Prophet Muḥammad (صَلَّى ٱللَّهُ عَلَيْهِ وَسَلَّمَ) and save him from all deficiency.

تم بحمد الله

APPENDIX

Translation of Sūrah Yūsuf

1. *Alif-Lām-Rā.* [These letters are one of the miracles of the Qur'ān, and none but Allāh (Alone) knows their meanings]. These are the Verses of the Clear Book (the Qur'ān that makes clear the legal and illegal things, legal laws, guidance and a blessing). [16]

2. Verily, We have sent it down as an Arabic Qur'ān in order that you may understand.

3. We relate unto you (Muḥammad) the best of stories through Our Revelations unto you, of this Qur'ān. And before this (i.e. before the coming of Divine Inspiration to you), you were among those who knew nothing about it (the Qur'ān).

---

[16] Translation by Dr. Muḥammad Taqi-ūd-Dīn al-Hilālī, Ph.D & Dr. Muḥammad Muḥsin Khān.

4. (Remember) when Yūsuf (Joseph) said to his father: "O my father! Verily, I saw (in a dream) eleven stars and the sun and the moon, I saw them prostrating themselves to me."

5. He (the father) said: "O' my son! Relate not your vision to your brothers, lest they arrange a plot against you. Verily! *Shaitān* (Satan) is to man an open enemy!"

6. "Thus will your Lord choose you and teach you the interpretation of dreams (and other things) and perfect His Favour on you and on the offspring of Ya'qūb (Jacob), as He perfected it on your fathers, Ibrāhīm (Abraham) and Ishāq (Isaac) aforetime! Verily, your Lord is All-Knowing, All-Wise."

7. Verily, in Yūsuf (Joseph) and his brethren, there were *Ayāt* (proofs, evidences, verses, lessons, signs, revelations, etc.) for those who ask.

8. When they said: "Truly, Yūsuf (Joseph) and his brother (Benjamin) are loved more by our father than we, but we are '*Usbaḥ* (a strong group). Really, our father is in a plain error."

9. "We will kill Yūsuf (Joseph) or cast him out to some (other) land, so that the favour of your father may be given to you alone, and after that you will be righteous folk (by intending repentance before committing the sin)."

10. One from among them said: "Kill not Yūsuf (Joseph), but if you must do something, throw him down to the bottom of a well, he will be picked up by some caravan of travellers."

11. They said: "O' our father! Why do you not trust us with Yūsuf (Joseph), - when we are indeed his well-wishers?"

12. "Send him with us tomorrow to enjoy himself and play, and verily, we will take care of him."

13. He [Ya'qūb (Jacob)] said: "Truly, it saddens me that you should take him away. I fear lest a wolf should devour him, while you are careless of him."

14. They said: "If a wolf devours him, while we are *'Usbah* (a strong group) (to guard him), then surely, we are the losers."

15. So, when they took him away, they all agreed to throw him down to the bottom of the well, and We inspired in him: "Indeed, you shall (one day) inform them of this their affair, when they know (you) not."

16. And they came to their father in the early part of the night weeping.

17. They said: "O' our father! We went racing with one another, and left Yūsuf (Joseph) by our belongings and a wolf devoured him; but you will never believe us even when we speak the truth."

18. And they brought his shirt stained with false blood. He said: "Nay, but your own selves have made up a tale. So (for me) patience is most fitting. And it is Allāh (Alone) Whose help can be sought against that which you assert."

19. And there came a caravan of travellers; they sent their water-drawer, and he let down his bucket (into the well). He said: "What good news! Here is a boy." So they hid him as merchandise (a slave). And Allāh was the All-Knower of what they did.

20. And they sold him for a low price, - for a few *Dirhams* (i.e. for a few silver coins). And they were of those who regarded him insignificant.

21. And he (the man) from Egypt who bought him, said to his wife: "Make his stay comfortable, maybe he will profit us or we shall adopt him as a son." Thus did We establish Yūsuf (Joseph) in the land, that We might teach him the interpretation of events. And Allāh has full power and control over His Affairs, but most of men know not.

22. And when he [Yūsuf (Joseph)] attained his full manhood, We gave him wisdom and knowledge (the Prophethood), thus We reward the *Muḥsinūn* (doers of good - see V.2:112).

23. And she, in whose house he was, sought to seduce him (to do an evil act), she closed the doors and said: "Come on, O' you." He said: "I seek refuge in Allāh (or Allāh forbid)! Truly, he (your husband) is my master! He made my stay agreeable! (So I will never betray him). Verily, the wrong will never be successful."

24. And indeed she did desire him and he would have inclined to her desire, had he not seen the evidence of his Lord. Thus it was, that We might turn away from him evil and illegal sexual intercourse. Surely, he was one of Our chosen, guided slaves.

25. So they raced with one another to the door, and she tore his shirt from the back. They both found her lord (i.e. her husband) at the door. She said: "What is the recompense (punishment) for him who intended an evil design against your wife, except that he be put in prison or a painful torment?"

26. He [Yūsuf (Joseph)] said: "It was she that sought to seduce me," - and a witness of her household bore witness (saying): "If it be that his shirt is torn from the front, then her tale is true and he is a liar!

27. "But if it be that his shirt is torn from the back, then she has told a lie and he is speaking the truth!"

28. So when he (her husband) saw his [(Yusuf's (Joseph)] shirt torn at the back; (her husband) said: "Surely, it is a plot of you women! Certainly mighty is your plot!

29. "O' Yūsuf (Joseph)! Turn away from this! (O' woman!) Ask forgiveness for your sin. Verily, you were of the sinful."

30. And women in the city said: "The wife of al-'Azīz is seeking to seduce her (slave) young man, indeed she loves him violently; verily we see her in plain error."

31. So when she heard of their accusation, she sent for them and prepared a banquet for them; she gave each one of them a knife (to cut the foodstuff with), and she said [(to Yūsuf (Joseph)]: "Come out before them." Then, when they saw him, they exalted him (at his beauty) and (in their astonishment) cut their hands. They said: "How perfect is Allāh (or Allāh forbid)! No man is this! This is none other than a noble angel!"

32. She said: "This is he (the young man) about whom you did blame me (for his love), and I did seek to seduce him, but he refused. And now if he refuses to obey my order, he shall certainly be cast into prison, and will be one of those who are disgraced."

33. He said: "O' my Lord! Prison is more to my liking than that to which they invite me. Unless You turn away their plot from me, I will feel inclined towards them and be one (of those who commit sin and deserve blame or those who do deeds) of the ignorant."

34. So his Lord answered his invocation and turned away from him their plot. Verily, He is the All-Hearer, the All-Knower.

35. Then it appeared to them, after they had seen the proofs (of his innocence) to imprison him for a time.

36. And there entered with him two young men in the prison. One of them said: "Verily, I saw myself (in a dream) pressing wine." The other said: "Verily, I saw myself (in a dream) carrying bread on my head and birds were eating thereof." (They said): "Inform us of the interpretation of this. Verily, we think you are one of the *Muhsinun* (doers of good)."

37. He said: "No food will come to you (in wakefulness or in dream) as your provision, but I will inform (in wakefulness) its interpretation before it (the food) comes. This is of that which my Lord has taught me. Verily, I have abandoned the religion of a people that believe not in Allāh and are disbelievers in the Hereafter (i.e. the *Kan'aniun* of Egypt who were polytheists and used to worship sun and other false deities).

38. "And I have followed the religion of my fathers - Ibrāhīm (Abraham), Ishāq (Isaac) and Ya'qūb (Jacob), and never could we attribute any partners whatsoever to Allāh. This is from the Grace of Allāh to us and to mankind, but most men thank not (i.e. they neither believe in Allāh, nor worship Him)."

39. "O' two companions of the prison! Are many different lords (gods) better or Allāh, the One, the Irresistible?"

40. "You do not worship besides Him but only names which you have named (forged) you and your fathers, for which Allāh has sent down no authority. The command (or the judgement) is for none but Allāh. He has commanded that you worship none but Him (i.e. His Monotheism), that is the (true) straight religion, but most men know not."

41. "O' two companions of the prison! As for one of you, he (as a servant) will pour out wine for his lord (king or master) to drink; and as for the other, he will be crucified and birds will eat from his head. Thus is the case judged concerning which you both did inquire."

42. And he said to the one whom he knew to be saved: "Mention me to your lord (i.e. your king, so as to get me out of the prison)." But *Shaitān* (Satan) made him forget to mention it to his Lord [or Satan made [(Yūsuf (Joseph)] to forget the remembrance of his Lord (Allāh) as to ask for His Help, instead of others]. So [Yūsuf (Joseph)] stayed in prison a few (more) years.

43. And the king (of Egypt) said: "Verily, I saw (in a dream) seven fat cows, whom seven lean ones were devouring - and of seven green ears of corn, and (seven) others dry. O' notables! Explain to me my dream, if it be that you can interpret dreams."

44. They said: "Mixed up false dreams and we are not skilled in the interpretation of dreams."

45. Then the man who was released (one of the two who were in prison), now at length remembered and said: "I will tell you its interpretation, so send me forth."

46. (He said): "O' Yūsuf (Joseph), the man of truth! Explain to us (the dream) of seven fat cows whom seven lean ones were devouring, and of seven green ears of corn, and (seven) others dry, that I may return to the people, and that they may know."

47. [(Yūsuf (Joseph)] said: "For seven consecutive years, you shall sow as usual and that (the harvest) which you reap you shall leave in ears, (all) - except a little of it which you may eat."

48. "Then will come after that, seven hard (years), which will devour what you have laid by in advance for them, (all) except a little of that which you have guarded (stored)."

49. "Then thereafter will come a year in which people will have abundant rain and in which they will press (wine and oil)."

50. And the king said: "Bring him to me." But when the messenger came to him, [Yūsuf (Joseph)] said: "Return to your lord and ask him, What happened to the women who cut their hands? Surely, my Lord (Allāh) is Well-Aware of their plot."

51. (The King) said (to the women): "What was your affair when you did seek to seduce Yūsuf (Joseph)?" The women said: "Allāh forbid! No evil know we against him! The wife of al-'Azīz said: "Now the truth is manifest (to all), it was I who sought to seduce him, and he is surely of the truthful."

52. [Then Yūsuf (Joseph) said: "I asked for this enquiry] in order that he (al-'Azīz) may know that I betrayed him not in secret. And, verily! Allāh guides not the plot of the betrayers.

53. "And I free not myself (from the blame). Verily, the (human) self is inclined to evil, except when my Lord bestows His Mercy (upon whom He wills). Verily, my Lord is Oft-Forgiving, Most Merciful."

54. And the king said: "Bring him to me that I may attach him to my person." Then, when he spoke to him, he said: "Verily, this day, you are with us high in rank and fully trusted."

55. [Yūsuf (Joseph)] said: "Set me over the storehouses of the land; I will indeed guard them with full knowledge" (as a minister of finance in Egypt, in place of al-'Azīz who was dead at that time).

56. Thus did We give full authority to Yūsuf (Joseph) in the land, to take possession therein, as when or where he likes. We bestow of Our Mercy on whom We please, and We make not to be lost the reward of *al-Muḥsinūn* (the good doers).

57. And verily, the reward of the Hereafter is better for those who believe and used to fear Allāh and keep their duty to Him (by abstaining from all kinds of sins and evil deeds and by performing all kinds of righteous good deeds).

58. And Yusuf's (Joseph) brethren came and they entered unto him, and he recognized them, but they recognized him not.

59. And when he had furnished them forth with provisions (according to their need), he said: "Bring me a brother of yours from your father; (he meant Benjamin). See you not that I give full measure, and that I am the best of the hosts?"

60. "But if you bring him not to me, there shall be no measure (of corn) for you with me, nor shall you come near me."

61. They said: "We shall try to get permission (for him) from his father, and verily, we shall do it."

62. And [Yūsuf (Joseph)] told his servants to put their money (with which they had bought the corn) into their bags, so that they might know it when they go back to their people, in order that they might come back.

63. So, when they returned to their father, they said: "O our father! No more measure of grain shall we get (unless we take our brother). So send our brother with us, and we shall get our measure and truly we will guard him."

64. He said: "Can I entrust him to you except as I entrusted his brother [Yūsuf (Joseph)] to you a foretime? But Allāh is the Best to guard, and He is the Most Merciful of those who show mercy."

65. And when they opened their bags, they found their money had been returned to them. They said: "O' our father! What (more) can we desire? This, our money has been returned to us, so we shall get (more) food for our family, and we shall guard our brother and add one more measure of a camel's load. This quantity is easy (for the king to give)."

66. He [Yaqūb (Jacob)] said: "I will not send him with you until you swear a solemn oath to me in Allāh's Name, that you will bring him back to me unless you are yourselves surrounded (by enemies, etc.)," And when they had sworn their solemn oath, he said: "Allāh is the Witness over what we have said."

67. And he said: "O' my sons! Do not enter by one gate, but enter by different gates, and I cannot avail you against Allāh at all. Verily! The decision rests only with Allāh. In him, I put my trust and let all those that trust, put their trust in Him."

68. And when they entered according to their father's advice, it did not avail them in the least against (the Will of) Allāh, it was but a need of Ya'qūb's (Jacob) inner-self which he discharged. And verily, he was endowed with knowledge because We had taught him, but most men know not.

69. And when they went in before Yūsuf (Joseph), he betook his brother (Benjamin) to himself and said: "Verily!I am your brother, so grieve not for what they used to do."

70. So when he had furnished them forth with their provisions, he put the (golden) bowl into his brother's bag, then a crier cried: "O you (in) the caravan! Surely, you are thieves!"

71. They, turning towards them, said: "What is it that you have missed?"

72. They said: "We have missed the (golden) bowl of the king and for him who produces it is (the reward of) a camel load; I will be bound by it."

73. They said: "By Allāh! Indeed you know that we came not to make mischief in the land, and we are no thieves!"

74. They [Yusuf's (Joseph) men] said: "What then shall be the penalty of him, if you are (proved to be) liars."

75. They [Yusuf's (Joseph) brothers] said: "The penalty should be that he, in whose bag it is found, should be held for the punishment (of the crime). Thus we punish the wrong-doers!"

76. So he [Yūsuf (Joseph)] began (the search) in their bags before the bag of his brother. Then he brought it out of his brother's bag. Thus did We plan for Yūsuf (Joseph). He could not take his brother by the law of the king (as a slave), except that Allāh willed it. (So Allāh made the brothers to bind themselves with their way of "punishment, i.e. enslaving of a thief.") We raise to degrees whom We please, but over all those endowed with knowledge is the All-Knowing (Allāh).

77. They [(Yusuf's (Joseph) brothers] said: "If he steals, there was a brother of his [Yūsuf (Joseph)] who did steal before (him)." But these things did Yūsuf (Joseph) keep in himself, revealing not the secrets to them. He said (within himself): "You are in worst case, and Allāh knows best the truth of what you assert!"

78. They said: "O' ruler of the land! Verily, he has an old father (who will grieve for him); so take one of us in his place. Indeed we think that you are one of the *Muḥsinūn* (good-doers - see V.2:112)."

79. He said: "Allāh forbid that we should take anyone but him with whom we found our property. Indeed (if we did so), we should be wrong-doers."

80. So, when they despaired of him, they held a conference in private. The eldest among them said: "Know you not that your father did take an oath from you in Allāh's Name, and before this you did fail in your duty with Yūsuf (Joseph)? Therefore I will not leave this land until my father permits me, or Allāh decides my case (by releasing Benjamin) and He is the Best of the judges."

81. "Return to your father and say, 'O' our father! Verily, your son (Benjamin) has stolen, and we testify not except according to what we know, and we could not know the unseen!"

82. And ask (the people of) the town where we have been, and the caravan in which we returned, and indeed we are telling the truth.

83. He [Ya'qūb (Jacob)] said: "Nay, but your ownselves have beguiled you into something. So patience is most fitting (for me). May be Allāh will bring them (back) all to me. Truly He is All-Knowing, All-Wise."

84. And he turned away from them and said: "Alas, my grief for Yūsuf (Joseph)!" And he lost his sight because of the sorrow that he was suppressing.

85. They said: "By Allāh! You will never cease remembering Yūsuf (Joseph) until you become weak with old age, or until you be of the dead."

86. He said: "I only complain of my grief and sorrow to Allāh, and I know from Allāh that which you know not.

87. "O' my sons! Go you and enquire about Yūsuf (Joseph) and his brother, and never give up hope of Allāh's Mercy. Certainly no one despairs of Allāh's Mercy, except the people who disbelieve."

88. Then, when they entered unto him [Yūsuf (Joseph)], they said: "O ruler of the land! A hard time has hit us and our family, and we have brought but poor capital, so pay us full measure and be charitable to us. Truly, Allāh does reward the charitable."

89. He said: "Do you know what you did with Yūsuf (Joseph) and his brother, when you were ignorant?"

90. They said: "Are you indeed Yūsuf (Joseph)?" He said: "I am Yūsuf (Joseph), and this is my brother (Benjamin). Allāh has indeed been gracious to us. Verily, he who fears Allāh with obedience to Him (by abstaining from sins and evil deeds, and by performing righteous good deeds), and is patient, then surely, Allāh makes not the reward of the *Muḥsinūn* (good-doers) to be lost."

91. They said: "By Allāh! Indeed Allāh has preferred you above us, and we certainly have been sinners."

92. He said: "No reproach on you this day, may Allāh forgive you, and He is the Most Merciful of those who show mercy!

93. "Go with this shirt of mine, and cast it over the face of my father, he will become clear-sighted, and bring to me all your family."

94. And when the caravan departed, their father said: "I do indeed feel the smell of Yūsuf (Joseph), if only you think me not a dotard (a person who has weakness of mind because of old age)."

95. They said: "By Allāh! Certainly, you are in your old error."

96. Then, when the bearer of the glad tidings arrived, he cast it (the shirt) over his face, and he became clear-sighted. He said: "Did I not say to you, 'I know from Allāh that which you know not.' "

97. They said: "O' our father! Ask forgiveness (from Allāh) for our sins, indeed we have been sinners."

98. He said: "I will ask my Lord for forgiveness for you, verily He! Only He is the Oft-Forgiving, the Most Merciful."

99. Then, when they entered unto Yūsuf (Joseph), he betook his parents to himself and said: "Enter Egypt, if Allāh wills, in security."

100. And he raised his parents to the throne and they fell down before him prostrate. And he said: "O' my father! This is the interpretation of my dream a foretime! My Lord has made it come true! He was indeed good to me, when He took me out of the prison, and brought you (all here) out of the bedouin-life, after *Shaitan* (Satan) had sown enmity between me and my brothers. Certainly, my Lord is the Most Courteous and Kind unto whom He will. Truly He! Only He is the All-Knowing, the All-Wise.

101. "My Lord! You have indeed bestowed on me of the sovereignty, and taught me the interpretation of dreams; The (only) Creator of the heavens and the earth! You are my *Wali* (Protector, Helper, Supporter, Guardian, etc.) in this world and in the Hereafter, cause me to die as a Muslim (the one submitting to Your Will), and join me with the righteous."

102. This is of the news of the *Ghaib* (unseen) which We reveal by Inspiration to you (O' Muḥammad). You were not (present) with them when they arranged their plan together, and (also, while) they were plotting.

103. And most of mankind will not believe even if you desire it eagerly.

104. And no reward you (O' Muḥammad) ask of them (those who deny your Prophethood) for it, it(the Qur'ān) is no less than a Reminder and an advice unto the *'Alamin* (men and *jinns*).

105. And how many a sign in the heavens and the earth they pass by, while they are averse therefrom.

106. And most of them believe not in Allāh except that they attribute partners unto Him [i.e. they are *Mushrikun* -polytheists - see Verse 6: 121].

107. Do they then feel secure from the coming against them of the covering veil of the Torment of Allāh, or of the coming against them of the (Final) Hour, all of a sudden while they perceive not?

108. Say (O' Muḥammad): "This is my way; I invite unto Allāh (i.e. to the Oneness of Allāh - Islamic Monotheism) with sure knowledge, I and whosoever follows me (also must invite others to Allāh i.e to the Oneness of Allāh - Islamic Monotheism) with sure knowledge. And Glorified and Exalted be Allāh (above all that they associate as partners with Him). And I am not of the *Mushrikun* (polytheists, pagans, idolaters and disbelievers in the Oneness of Allāh; those who worship others along with Allāh or set up rivals or partners to Allāh)."

109. And We sent not before you (as Messengers) any but men, whom We inspired from among the people of townships. Have they not travelled through the earth and seen what was the end of those who were before them? And verily, the home of the Hereafter is the best for those who fear Allāh and obey Him (by abstaining from sins and evil deeds, and by performing righteous good deeds). Do you not then understand?

110. (They were reprieved) until, when the Messengers gave up hope and thought that they were denied (by their people), then came to them Our Help, and whomsoever We willed were delivered. And Our Punishment cannot be warded off from the people who are *Mujrimun* (criminals, disobedient to Allāh, sinners, disbelievers, polytheists).

111. Indeed in their stories, there is a lesson for men of understanding. It (the Qur'ān) is not a forged statement but a confirmation of the Allāh's existing Books [the *Taurāt* (Torah), the *Injīl* (Gospel) and other Scriptures of Allāh] and a detailed explanation of everything and a guide and a Mercy for the people who believe.

الفهرس

General Indexes

Index of Arabic Terms

al-Asbāṭ	Abū al-'Aliyah, ar-Rabī' and Qaṭadah said, *al-Asbāṭ* are the twelve sons of Ya'qūb, and each one of them had an *Ummah* of people from his descendants. This is why they were called *al-Asbawṭ*. al-Khalīl ibn Aḥmad and others said, *al-Asbāṭ* among the Children of Isrā'īl are just like the tribes among the Children of Ismā'īl.' This means that *al-Asbāṭ* are the various tribes of the Children of Israel, among whom Allah sent several Prophets. Musá said to the Children of Isrā'īl.
al-Qaṣīm	One of the thirteen administrative regions of Saudi Arabia.
Ḥadīth	The term applied to specific reports of the prophet Muḥammad's

	(صَلَّى ٱللَّهُ عَلَيْهِ وَسَلَّمَ) words, actions and silent approvals.
Jāhiliyah	Pre-Islāmic period of ignorance before the advent of Prophet Muḥammad (صَلَّى ٱللَّهُ عَلَيْهِ وَسَلَّمَ).
Muhājirūn	*Lit;* migrants. The citizens of Mekkah that migrated to the city of Madinah.
Salaf as- Ṣālih	*Lit;* the Pious Predecessors. The technical term used in reference to the first three generations of the Islāmic *Ummah*.
Salafī	A follower of the first three generations of the Islāmic *Ummah*.
Shām	The historic geographic region of Syria or Greater Syria often called Syria-Palestine or the Levant in modern literature, and *Shām* in traditional Arabic and Islamic literature.
Sunan	See *Sunnah*.
Sunnah	*Lit;* way, path. *pl*; *Sunnan.* The actions and statements and silent approvals of the Prophet Muḥammad (صَلَّى ٱللَّهُ عَلَيْهِ وَسَلَّمَ) that have been reported in authentic *ḥadīths*.

Tābiʿūn — *Lit; the followers.* The generation that followed the era of the Prophet (ﷺ) and the Companion.

Taqwā — *Lit;* the fear of Allāh (تَبَارَكَ وَتَعَالَى). Talq Ibn Habīd said: *Taqwā* is that you act in obedience to Allāh (تَبَارَكَ وَتَعَالَى), and hope in His Mercy, upon a light from Him; and *Taqwā* is leaving acts of disobedience to Allāh (تَبَارَكَ وَتَعَالَى) out of fear of Him, upon a light from Him. See Ibn Abī Shaybāh in *Kitāb al-Imān* (no: 99).

Tawḥīd — *Lit*; monotheism, unification. To absolutely single out Allāh (تَبَارَكَ وَتَعَالَى) in His Worship, Lordship and Names and Attributes. It is to make all of your worship solely for Allāh (تَبَارَكَ وَتَعَالَى).

Our Da'wāh

1. We believe in Allāh and His Names and Attributes (تَبَارَكَ وَتَعَالَى), as they were mentioned in the Book of Allāh (تَبَارَكَ وَتَعَالَى) and in the *Sunnah* of the Messenger of Allāh (صَلَّى ٱللَّهُ عَلَيْهِ وَسَلَّمَ), without *tahrīf* (distortion), nor *ta'wīl* (figurative interpretation), nor *tamthīl* (making a likeness), nor *tashbīh* (resemblance), nor *ta'tīl* (denial).

2. We love the Companions of the Messenger of Allāh (صَلَّى ٱللَّهُ عَلَيْهِ وَسَلَّمَ), and we hate those who speak against them. We believe that to speak ill of them is to speak ill of the Religion, because they are the ones who conveyed it to us. And we love the Family of the Prophet (صَلَّى ٱللَّهُ عَلَيْهِ وَسَلَّمَ) with love that is permitted by the Islamic legislation.

3. We love the People of *Ḥadīth* and all of the *Salaf* of the *Ummah* from *Ahlus-Sunnah*.

4. We despise *'Ilm ul-kalām* (rhetoric theological), and we view it to be from amongst the greatest reasons for the division in the *Ummah*.[17]

5. We do not accept anything from the books of *fiqh* (jurisprudence), nor from the books of *tafsīr* (explanation of the Qur'ān), nor from the ancient stories, nor from the *Sīrah* (biography) of the Prophet (صَلَّى ٱللَّهُ عَلَيْهِ وَسَلَّمَ), except that which has been confirmed from Allāh (تَبَارَكَ وَتَعَالَىٰ) or from His Messenger (صَلَّى ٱللَّهُ عَلَيْهِ وَسَلَّمَ). We do not mean that we have rejected them, nor do we claim that we are not in need of them. Rather, we benefit from the discoveries of our Scholars and the jurists and other than them. However, we do not accept a ruling, except with an authentic proof.

6. We do not write in our books, nor do we cover in our lessons, nor do we give sermons with anything except the Qur'ān, or the authentic and authoritative *ḥadīth*. And we detest what emanates from many books and admonishers in terms of false stories and weak and fabricated *ḥadīths*.

7. We do not perform *takfīr* (excommunication) upon any Muslim due to any sin, except *Shirk* (polytheism) with Allāh (تَبَارَكَ وَتَعَالَىٰ), or the abandonment of Prayer, or apostasy. We seek refuge in Allāh (تَبَارَكَ وَتَعَالَىٰ) from that.

8. We believe that the Qur'ān is the Speech of Allāh (تَبَارَكَ وَتَعَالَىٰ), it is not created.

---

[17] **[TN]**: Imām ash-Shāfi'ī (رَحِمَهُ ٱللَّهُ) said: "My verdict on the people of *kalām* (kalāmists) is that they should be placed upon a domesticated donkey, and led around the Bedouin clans and tribes while it is announced publicly that this is the reward of those who reject the Book of Allāh, and busy themselves with rhetoric (*kalām*)."[17] See Ibn 'Abī al-'Izz, *Sharḥ al-'Aqīdah aṭ-Ṭaḥāwiyyah*' (p.75).

9. We hold that our obligation is to co-operate with the group that follows the methodology of the Book and the *Sunnah,* and what the *Salaf* of the *Ummah* were upon; in terms of calling to Allāh (تَبَارَكَ وَتَعَالَى) the Glorified, and being sincere in worship of Him, and warning from *Shirk*, innovations, and disobedience, and to advise all of the groups that oppose this. So co-operating upon righteousness and piety (*taqwā*) and mutual advising necessitates warning against evil and not co-operating with the wicked.

10. We do not deem it correct to revolt against the rulers, nor do we feel that revolutions bring about reconciliation. Rather, they corrupt the community.

11. We hold that this multiplicity of present day parties is a reason for the division of the Muslims and their weakness. So therefore we set about freeing the minds from the fetters of blind-following and the darkness of sectarianism and party spirit.

12. We restrict our understanding of the Book of Allāh (تَبَارَكَ وَتَعَالَى) and the *Sunnah* of the Messenger of Allāh (صَلَّى ٱللَّهُ عَلَيْهِ وَسَلَّمَ) to the understanding of the *Salaf* of the *Ummah* from the Scholars of *ḥadīth*, not the blind-followers of their individuals. Rather, we take the truth from wherever it comes. And we know that there are those who claim *Salafiyyah*, yet *Salafiyyah* is free from them, since they bring to the society what Allāh (تَبَارَكَ وَتَعَالَى) has prohibited.

13. We believe in 'cultivating the young generation upon this Islam, purified from all that we have mentioned, giving to them a correct Islāmic education from the start - without any influence from the disbelieving western education.

14. We believe that politics is a part of the Religion, and those who try to separate the Religion from politics are only attempting to destroy the Religion and to spread chaos.

15. We believe that there will be no honour or victory for the Muslims until they return to the Book of Allāh (تَبَارَكَ وَتَعَالَىٰ) and to the *Sunnah* of the Messenger of Allāh (صَلَّى ٱللَّهُ عَلَيْهِ وَسَلَّمَ).

16. We oppose those who divide the Religion into trivialities and important issues. And we know that this is a destructive *da'wāh*.

17. We oppose those who put down the knowledge of the *Sunnah*, and say that this is not the time for it. Likewise, we oppose those who put down acting upon the *Sunnah* of the Messenger of Allāh (صَلَّى ٱللَّهُ عَلَيْهِ وَسَلَّمَ).

18. Our *da'wāh* and our *'aqīdah* is more beloved to us than our own selves, our wealth and our offspring. So we are not prepared to part with it for gold nor silver. We say this so that no one may have hope in buying out our *da'wāh*, nor should he think that it is possible for him to purchase it from us for *dīnār* or *dirham*.

19. We love the present day Scholars of the *Sunnah* and hope to benefit from them and regret the passing away of many of them.

20. We do not accept a *fatwā* except from the Book of Allāh (تَبَارَكَ وَتَعَالَىٰ) and the *Sunnah* of the Messenger of Allāh (صَلَّى ٱللَّهُ عَلَيْهِ وَسَلَّمَ).

These are glimpses into our *'aqīdah* and our *da'wāh*. So if one has any objection to this, then we are prepared to accept advice if it is truthful, and to refute it if it is erroneous, and to avoid it if it is stubborn rejection. And Allāh (تَبَارَكَ وَتَعَالَىٰ) knows best.[18]

[18] Summarised from *Tarjumah Abī 'Abd ur-Raḥmān Muqbil ibn Ḥādī al-Wādi'ī* (p. 135-142) of Shaykh Muqbil Ibn Hādī al-Wādi'ī.